Looking Unto Jesus

Looking Unto Jesus

The Hope from One Generation to the Next

Wayne Bills

Copyright © 2010 by Wayne Bills.

Library of Congress Control Number:		2010911615
ISBN:	Hardcover	978-1-4535-5407-4
	Softcover	978-1-4535-5406-7
	Ebook	978-1-4535-5408-1

All rights reserved. No part of this book may be reproduced or transmitted in any form or by any means, electronic or mechanical, including photocopying, recording, or by any information storage and retrieval system, without permission in writing from the copyright owner.

This book was printed in the United States of America.

To order additional copies of this book, contact:
Xlibris Corporation
1-888-795-4274
www.Xlibris.com
Orders@Xlibris.com
84563

Contents

Abortion Cry 9
Opportunities Will Catch Us By Surprise! 10
Thinkers Thoughts That Go Unspoken 12
There Is No Place To Go But On Your Knees 14
Everything Comes With Consequences 16
Don't Try To Put A Ocean Liner In A Creek 17
Mama's Old Beat Up Wash Tub 18
As If A New Boast 20
A Poet 21
"I Am" 22
"Let It Be" 23
It's All For You 24
He ever Goes Before Us 25
Hurricane Force 26
The In-Growing Of Time Is Short Lived 28
Contentment: One Moment Please! 30
In The Bond Of Love 31
Who Is He That Teaches . . . Who Is He That Learns 32
Three Bearing Witness 33
I Have Set My Face Like A Flint 35
"It Is Written" 36
Conscience 37
Leaving Nothing Behind 38
Let Us Go You And I 39
As Sure As Sure Can Be 40
In the Face of the Clock 41

Thanksgiving Prayer 42
"As Leaves Fall" 43
The Caring Desire That Always Makes A Difference 44
The Silence Garden Of Life..45
Common People Ordinary Things 46
Love Remembers 47
The Known And The Unknown 48
The King Is Coming! 49
Get Up And Win The Race..50
The Divine Grip Of Grace 51
The Holy Divine Grip Of Amazing Grace.................................52
Basic Endless Endurance (Happy Easter)...................................53
The right to life..54
Make Us Lord, So Like You...55
Forever Grateful 57
Make Available 58
Ascribe Unto The Lord...59
Before We Be No More 60
A Personal Choice 61
Motive More Meaningful 63
Taste the air..64
Only One Answer 66
May The Word Of God Bless Us..67
JESUS Came And HE Is Risen!..68
Luke 10:20 JUBILEE!...69
We Unto Jesus, Jesus Unto His Father 70
Walk Before God..71
Shine! Shine! Shine!...72
Faces of our hearts (OUR GLORIOUS) 73
The Gospel 74
Against the odds...75
Deliberate The Origin And Design Of A Pearl 76
Mastering the notes 77

Keep praying	79
Numbering Our Days	80
No Greater Love	81
Riches (Wisdom From Above)	82
Bright Morning Star	83
Purchased . . . Made Closer To Him (Touching Jesus Is All That Matters)	84
Valley Of Dreams (Keeping The Spark)	85
Bidden to Come	86
To My Children *(I Wish You Love)*	87
I Can Feel You My Lord Breathing	88
In The Hands Of Our Lord	89
Jesus . . . is Love In Any Language	90
The Sinner's Prayer	91
Trip Of My Life Time	92
My Faith Defines Who I Am . .	93
Face Down Again	94
Jesus Saves!!!	95
Widen Our Vision	96
Love His Salvation	97
Happy 2008 ISRAEL Sixtieth Up To: Jerusalem! (The White Stone)	98
Moving The Mountain	99
Shining Shield! And Shining Sword!	100
ISRAEL, Holy Ground	101
Feeling Jesus' Warmth!!!	102
Forgiveness!!!	103
Godhearted Clothed Multitude HEB. 12:1, 2	105
Our Faith In JESUS Still Gentle Voice I Pet. 5:6,7; 2 COR. 12:9	107
ISRAEL! The Holy Ground! PS. 122	110

Feeling Jesus Warmth!!! Luke 24:32
   Joy In The Lord Jesus Always!..112
Via Dolorosa!!!
   Isaiah 53..114
Hand Grafted In At The Seams
   Matt. 6:33..115
Songs Of Deliverance And Mercy!
   Ps. 32:7, 8, 10, 11 116
Real Heartfelt Love In The Proven Holy Word Of God
   (Ps. 119) (The Way Of The Cross!) 118
O Jerusalem Jerusalem Jerusalem..121
Victory Unto Victory!!!
   (Exo. 14:14 2 Cor. 12:9) 122
When Our Delight And Joy Is In Jesus
   PSALM 37:3-5..124
Then Came The Morning In Jerusalem!
   Heb. 10:20 126
Happy 2008 Israel Sixtieth
   (Up To Jerusalem! ISA.62)..127
Appreciate And Be Grateful For 128
Appreciate And Be Grateful!!!
   I COR. 15:51-58 129
Jesus . . . lord Of New Life!!!..131
The Way Of Holiness!!!..132
Never Before 133
I'm In The Blood
   Gal. 6:14-Rom. 8 (Isa. 53 . . . via Dolorosa) 135
Daily Results Of Hope And Blessings Over The Years 137
Daily Inspired 139
Your Heart Soars In Jerusalem,
   ISA. 51:..141
The Day Of The Lord..145

Abortion Cry

O Mother, I just want you to know: I'm so sorry I can't be with you. The desire of life was so real to me. I knew every tear you cried, I was so much a part of you, I felt every pain you felt. And I just loved hearing your voice, I felt I was really beginning to know you.

O Mother, I felt so safe and protected: I didn't see how anything could go wrong. Everything seemed so wonderful and peaceful. Words just can't tell you how real each moment of life was to me. There was no hint that a cruel evil intruder could enter such a wonderful and peaceful place. No not even a hint.

O Mother, I wanted so much to love you: I had so much love to give you. I really believe with that love I had for you, together we could have overcome any and all your fears and imaginations. I really and truly believe I could have helped you love me.

O Mother, that cruel evil intruder had no pity, no mercy and no compassion.
I screamed! MOTHER!
But you didn't hear me.

O Mother, ask Jesus into your heart now. He has so much love to give you. For he promises we can overcome and he will never leave you or forsake you.

O Mother, let his sweet loving power touch you and make you whole.

Opportunities Will Catch Us By Surprise!

Heroes and heroics: Identify with opportunities others only dream
about. Seized by the moment, not intimidated, but instead in the heat
of emotions with the burning desire to respond, to defend the
defenseless, having a strong determination of resolve, to enter into
controversy or maybe attempt what nobody else thought possible,
therein giving voice to the injustices.

Heroes and heroics: To every action there is a reaction,
or the action
Goes unchecked. Like the story of David and Goliath: David didn't
come to camp to become a hero, he was bringing bread to his
brothers. Though he did identify with opportunities,
he was not
intimidated by the size of the giant. He entered into the controversy
with heroics, therein giving voice to the injustices.

Heroes and heroics: Being active helps us to be ready
and effective,
responsive and perceptive to what is going on around us
each day. By

being attentive, opportunities will not pass us by, as we grab
hold of
the moment, to establish what needs to be done.
All progress starts
with the first step, only then can it become the future giving
voice to
the injustices

Thinkers Thoughts That Go Unspoken

Thinkers Thoughts That Go Unspoken

In the quandary of unspoken thoughts, where the solo performance
meets head on with the numerous possibilities and responsibilities of inspecting, sorting out, classification, etc. Relaying along the delivery route of progress, the description portrayable path of movement will take it. Like a relay race, a race between two or three teams, in which each team member runs only a set part of
the race, and then is relieved by another member of the team.

In the quandary of unspoken thoughts where the solo performance encounters and undergoes difficulties, uneasiness, and perplexity, much like the lump that comes up in our throat, and we undersell the value of our quality, we know we are standing up on the inside, but we have the feeling of falling down on the outside . . . much like
the Spirit is
strong but the flesh is weak. Our predicament in this unpleasantness often brings with it a feeling of offense or wrongdoing, sometimes ridicule, followed by a remorseful awareness.

In the quandary of unspoken thoughts, we've got a friend; no matter how far gone we may feel, we are not beyond His reach. Though our Friend's foresight is all knowing and all-Powerful . . . our foresight remains forever unclear and fragile with our hindsight at 20-20. The awesome wonder of it all is that HIS AMAZING GRACE overlooks our frailness and vulnerability and continues to reach His hand out in help!

There Is No Place To Go But On Your Knees

When our hearts are quickened,
there is no place to go but on our knees.
When troubles weigh us down,
there is no place to go but on our knees.
When we suffer a great loss,
there is no place to go but on our knees.
When we feel empty,
there is no place to go but on our knees.
When guilt robs our joy,
there is no place to go but on our knees.
When we are face to face with the impossible,
there is no place to go but on our knees.
When we are burdened by anything,
there is no place to go but on our knees.
When we seek true purpose in life,
there is no place to go but on our knees.
When we desire Divine Love,
there is no place to go but on our knees.
When we need peace within,
there is no place to go but on our knees.
When we are trying to make sense of it all,
there is no place to go but on our knees.

When we a need a cleansing inner bath,
there is no place to go but on our knees.
When we wait upon the Lord in earnest,
there is no place to go but on our knees.
When we want the very best of all possibilities,
with all sufficiency, there is no place to go but on our knees.

Everything Comes With Consequences

In the evidence of data, by which proof or
probability may be established . . .
Everything comes with consequences.
In general life, to a regular person, factors
or development may indicate ones suitable action
or reaction connected with ones lifestyle . . .
Everything comes with consequences.
Eve had two sons, Abel kept sheep and Cain was
a tiller of the ground. In the process of time,
Cain brought an offering of fruit unto the LORD;
his brother Abel brought the firstborn of his flock
as an offering to the LORD. Jealousy erupted
between Cain and Abel when God had no respect for
Cain's offering while He did respect Abel's offering.
Upon God seeing the look of anger and rage
on Cain's face, and His knowing what
Cain intended to do to Abel, God warned Cain of
the pending consequences for any murderous
actions. Eventually, Cain did kill his brother
and did, indeed, suffer the consequences
God had forewarned him about.
In the relationship of important facts or considerations,
pertaining to any given moment,
Everything comes with consequences.
In examination, one can learn from another's consequences
to avoid unpleasing predicaments;
Of course to God be the glory.

Don't Try To Put A Ocean Liner In A Creek

Don't Try To Put An Ocean Liner In A Creek

We have to face it; there just some things we can't do.
    It's just not going to float.
We have to face it; things we plan don't always work out.
    It's just not going to float.
We have to face it; we can't relive that which is behind us.
    It's just not going to float.
We have to face it; we can't make tomorrow come sooner.
    It's just not going to float.

Mama's Old Beat Up Wash Tub

MAMA'S OLD BEAT UP WASHTUB . . .

If there was one memory that really stands out, I recall
of all my
younger childhood days.
It would be mama's old beat up washtub . . .

If there was dirty clothes to soak over night, wash
and rinse three
times, the next morning.
It would be mama's old beat up washtub . . .

If there was a wind out of the west or east, sound like someone
beating the back door down.
It would be mama's old beat up washtub . . .

If there was steam coming from the tub in the middle of floor,
it was
time to take a bath again.
It would be mama's old beat up washtub . . .

If there was a mark of 15.5 Gal on your bottom,
mama would laugh
as she dried you off.
It would be mama's old beat up washtub . . . .

If there was one thing hanging by the back door,
that we always
noticed, going out or coming in.
It would be mama's old beat up washtub.

As If A New Boast . . .

The night is now gone, what is that which stands before us?
Already busy traffic on the street below, meeting one with the other,
as they hurry in different directions.
As If A New Boast . . .

The night is now gone, what is that which stands before us?
Already the interrupted darkness that had been on the
street below, an inviting light to see a new day.
As If A New Boast . . .

The night is now gone, what is that which stands before us?
Already the birds are singing cheerfully on the street below,
an inviting tone to begin a new day.
As If A New Boast . . .

The night is now gone, what is that which stands before us?
Already the smell of pine trees in the air on the street below,
an inviting fragrance to savor a new day.
As If A New Boast . . .

The night is now gone, what is that which stands before us?
Already the warmth in the breeze on the street below,
an inviting gentle welcome, to touch a new day.
As If A New Boast . . .

A Poet

To start from a blank piece of paper and to offer ones expressions
to be reviewed,
not knowing if; to present in words will gain an audience,
or just have a special meaning only to ones self.

As the expressions begins to become spontaneous,
a kind of self-generated impulse, Interaction, from one
expression to the next, in harmony with what has been expressed
and will be expressed.

Much like pieces of a puzzle are laid out on a table,
a poet puts the pieces together,
each piece that fits another to make the picture.

A poet desires to leave a part of ones self, a sort of
Immortality, or
maybe just a mirror of that moment of time, the need
to fill the
blanks with ones own expressions.

"I Am"

I dance throughout the wheat fields, the wheat bows
and gestures,
as I leap and skip about excitingly.

I fly high upon the mountaintop, to share my strength,
the mountain
does tremble, under my power.

I walk on the storm clouds, to show my status to my would be
opposers, they faint for fear of my posture.

I meet with the deep to impart my wisdom, as I search out, to
remain, and hold on, to all that abides.

I breathe in the nostril of every living thing, LIFE to grant my
display ever before you, my awesomeness, that "I AM"
there is no
other.

"Let It Be"

Everything has a pattern, that's the way it is and the way it remains. Seed was in itself, after his kind . . .

The process came from an intelligence, with a will to cause what was desired." Let it be."
The issues of process unquestionably and absolutely begin and carry through to completion:
That is why process come with a duty and requirements.
That is why the sense of an obligation of binding duty to completion, is so sure and correct. (for failure to comply, to requirements is vain and foolishness.) "LET IT BE"

It's All For You

Someday Somewhere we can embrace and never let go.
Someday Somewhere we will know our place to fit.
Someday Somewhere all things work out for the best.
Someday Somewhere we can sing for sure joy.
Someday Somewhere it's all for you.

Someday Somewhere we can get closer and closer.
Someday Somewhere we will know our portion.
Someday Somewhere all things will be accomplished.
Someday Somewhere we can give our melody.
Someday Somewhere it's all for you.

Someday Somewhere we can show our affections
Someday Somewhere we will know our function.
Someday Somewhere all things will be pleasing.
Someday Somewhere nothing will be in vain.
Someday Somewhere it's all for you.

He ever Goes Before Us

We never know when He might intervene on our behalf today
We never know what His interest of in lighting us may be today.
We never know what His in tented purpose may be for us today.
We never know how He might want us to be a blessing today.
He ever goes before us.

We never know what doors He may open for us today.
We never know what doors He may close for us today.
We never know what advantage He may give us today.
We never know how He will lovingly benefit us today.
He ever goes before us.

We never know the battles He will win for us today.
We never know how He may suddenly enable us today.
We never know His effectiveness in our day today
We never know the real difference He makes today.
He ever goes before us.

Hurricane Force

Trapped in a Hurricane Force, nothing but dark black
over head.
Straight wind and water push the boat north and northeast.
Now the dark black waves are becoming rounding mountains;
it's hard to tell the water beneath from the sky above.
As the boat falls down, down, down; doom is on every side.

A man is asleep down below!.
What? What did you say? A man is asleep?
How? How could a man sleep in this hurricane force?
Who? Who is this man? Who is this man that knows no fear?
When doom is on every side. And our death undoubtedly
is so near.

Hurry, come, let us go wake him, so he will know our fate..
Wake up, wake up, don't you care we are going to die!
Now we see.
Yes, more clearly: He Cares! Now we see; we were the
ones asleep.
Now that it's all passed. Even the hurricane force obeys
His voice.
as He speaks to the storms of our lives, "PEACE, BE STILL"

Firmly and with confidence, He makes the sun want to shine
in our lives.
Ever with Unquestionable forbearance, waiting for the
opportune moment,

He constantly shows us His gentleness. He knows what
concerns us as we
live day to day. Storms they come and they go. Yet, day by day,
because of
His faithfulness and because of His compassions that never fail,
He remains
the same.

He is our joy spring of a new and living way, without Him we
can do nothing.
He is not asleep, we are the ones asleep. We are so asleep
in ourselves
and in our own journey we fail to notice He is the
continuous passage
ahead of us. Now, while there is still time to shine,
while it is still
called TODAY, may we Humble ourselves under the
mighty hand
of the Lord, that He might exalt us in due time as we
cast our cares
upon Him, our daily help, through the hurricane force of life.

The In-Growing Of Time Is Short Lived

There is an in-growing within through out our lives which becomes visible and plainly seen, as we age, from one appearance
to the next. From the time we are born there is a slow process of death's grip taking progress. There are times in our lives the progress seems to be inactive, as we try to hold on to a moment of jubilation. But, like grains of sand, the events of our lives
slip and slide through our fingers, as the in-growing of time is short lived.

There is also an in-growing outwardly through our lives which also
becomes visible and plainly seen, as we age, from one appearance
to the next. There are times in our lives when this progress seems
also to be inactive, as our inner strength and strong determination will
move us toward our clash. But like a strong fortress that wins battle after battle is laid to waste and deteriorates, the in-growing of time is short lived.

There is a growing within and without, and is visible and plainly
seen all around us. Young and old, strong and weak,
life and death; and even the strong sometimes die young . . .
One thing we learn through life is that life is fragile.
The days we have are numbered and are rapidly fading
into the past as we
live one day at a time. What we do with today is
what is required,
as the in-growing of time is short lived.

Contentment: One Moment Please!

The available seems to be just beyond us, hope in our journey with anticipation of a new moment to pierce through the high latitude.

Like an eagle, we desire to spread our wings and soar through the heavens . . . to come together with a great group of eagles with piercing screams of united joy.

Neither turning to the right nor to the left; looking straight ahead with expectations of a great, great, great feast, which is available just beyond us.

The consciousness of an endless yearning pain, with continuous movement toward becoming recreated and reinstated, till we all are filled with joy as we each come together just beyond us. What a moment that will be!

Whereas we shall all be changed, as in a moment or in the twinkling of an eye.
CONTENTMENT: ONE MOMENT PLEASE!

In The Bond Of Love

Love is a forbearing ability of tolerance . . . Love's endurance of pain, misery, and total failure is uncountable because they are unable to be counted in the bond of love.

The unmerited favorability of kindness . . . Love's superior quality appointing the basis of merit advancement because they are undeserved, or freely given, in the bond of love.

The contentment ability of gentleness . . . Love's desired possessions furnished to exercise pleasing advantageous honor, easy to handle, or manage in the bond of love.

The calming ability of peacefulness . . . Love's composed undisturbed advantage to help is not easily provoked and is not easily puffed up with pride in the bond of love.

The generous ability of unselfishness . . . Love's willing behavior to share and be concerned by participating in an effort of involvement to lend support in the bond of love.

The renewing ability of built-in permanent quality . . . Love's far superior attributes, a distinctive feature that identifies the way of life is above the wise in the bond of love.

Who Is He That Teaches . . .
Who Is He That Learns . . .

Genuine or artificial, actual or alleged . . . The adopted meaning of any interpretation formed as if it were to cause predicted results.
Meaningful or imitation, natural or counterfeit . . .
What something represents to the end of it's significance, tells us one way as well as the other.
THERE IS NO WISDOM . . . AGAINST GOD !!!

Certainty or presumption, merited or without proof . . .
Things that are certain occur day by day, in it's act of an unchanged form evidence, clear and obvious.
THERE IS NO WISDOM . . . AGAINST GOD !!!

Seasons come, Seasons go . . .
Is there a single clue, the grass withers and dies. The tree's leaves dry and fall, we know winter is coming. Is there a single clue, the grass shots up again. The tree's leaves grow back. We know spring is here.
THERE IS NO WISDOM . . . AGAINST GOD !!!

Three Bearing Witness

Many stories have all been told . . . Many stories the earth unfolds. Many stories the earth still holds.

Many stories have all been told . . . Many stories the seas unfolds. Many stories the sea still holds.

Many stories have all been told . . . Many stories that heaven unfolds. Many stories that heaven still holds.

The Earth, The Sea, The Heaven. Three Bearing Witness.

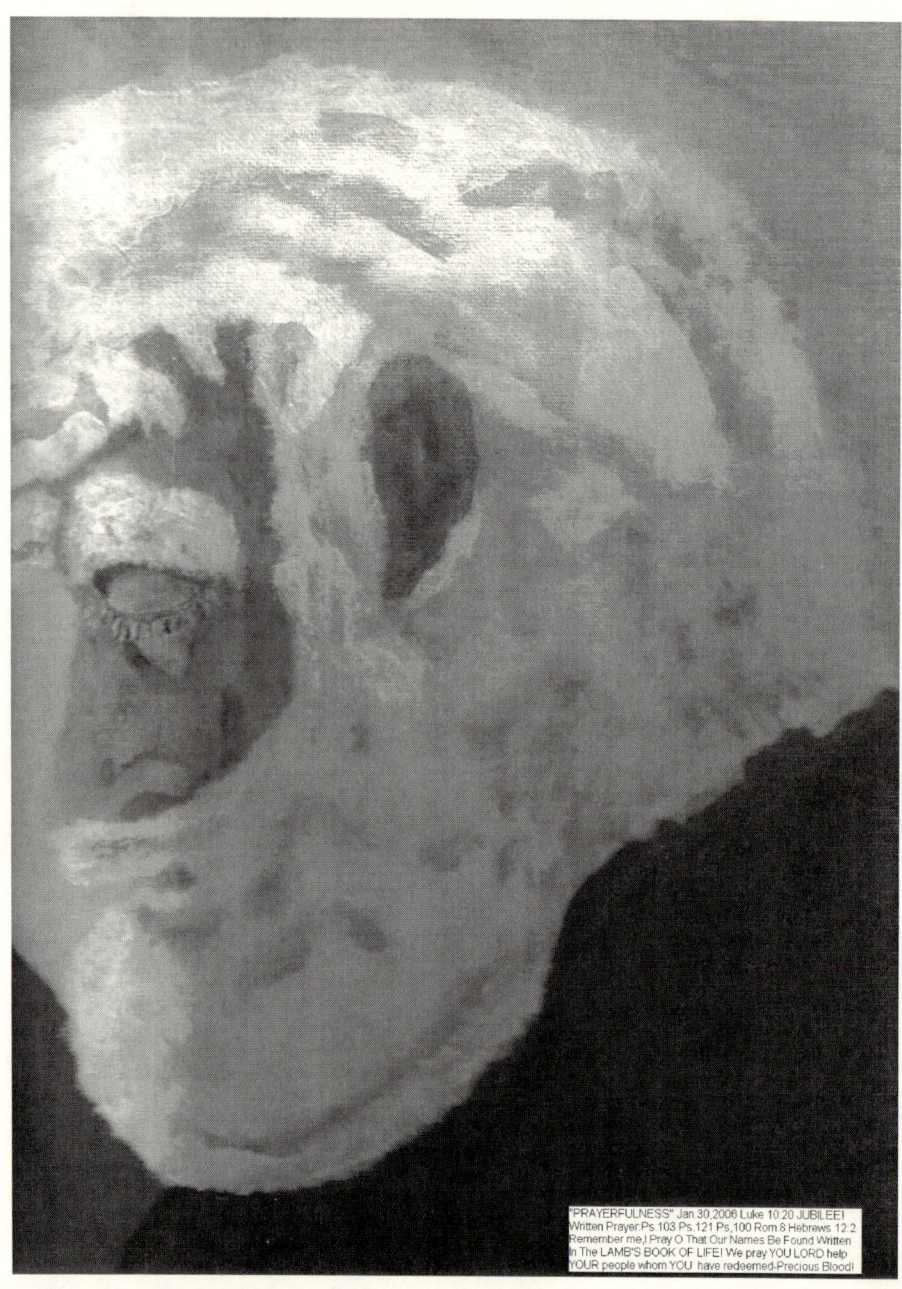

I Have Set My Face Like A Flint

(SOME DAY I WILL LAY DOWN MY CROSS AND GO HOME)

O LORD, Lead me in Thy righteous judgments and
daily establish Thy Way firmly in front of my face.
O LORD, Thou are the hope from one generation
unto the next. Even So . . . LORD JESUS >>> COME

I have set my face like a flint, God is all together good;
and His faithfulness is great to all generations . . .
Another time, another place when I at last see
Jesus' face. Where Jesus praise goes on and on and on.

JESUS presence shall fill every song of the blood bought.
His face will capture all tears and no more mourning. In joy
Then I will know He saw me too, and I was never out of His
care. I have set-up my banners In The Name Of THE LORD.

"It Is Written"

Shall we be overtaken of things that are
Continuous and having no part missing
Shall the limitations to become a part of; no longer
impose it's handicap to reach the once impossible?

As a moving finger writes, and having been written
moves continually to the following words.
Written words of silence speech that tears fall upon,
however what is written is written and not to be washed away.

Shall the words fill all necessity . . .
having energy to seek, find, and restore?
Shall the edges of each word know the secrets
and plans to insure it's success to the fullest?

To instill the very best gradually or directly, by moving on
to the next necessity.
Being able to discern every concealed thought and intention.

Shall great and wonderful things delight our eyes and
hearts as THE WORDS have promised?
Shall we all agree together for the first time, that all is
right, and we are secure from all wrong?
Shall we all joyfully partake of the tree of eternal life?

Conscience

Our being tender with the young.
Our being compassionate with the aged.
Our being sympathetic with the hurting.
Our being kind and tolerant to all.
Remembering God's mercy is new every morning.

For our conscience sake, hating no one.
For our conscience sake, spiting no one.
For our conscience sake, envying no one.
For our conscience sake, forbearing one another.
Remembering God's mercy is new every morning.

Pursuing peace with believing
for the best each new day.
Pursuing faith to carry on courageously,
each new day.
Pursuing hope of that which is hoped for,
each new day.
Pursuing a pure conscience
before God and man.
Remembering God's mercy
is new every morning.

Leaving Nothing Behind

Changing common actions of life toward positive tone to improve mildly, kindheartedly, but seriously that which has been forgotten or disregarded.

Life is passing swiftly, fading quickly, and consumed away, leaving nothing behind but the regrets of hollow choices and failures.

Life is in a measure, which signifies recourses and resources, and a means of actions effect, which is every possible behavior and possible motivational end result.

Life is both up and down, as they say, such is life . . . pick yourself up, get back into the race, and run with endurance to the finish line.

No life shall glorify or boast in itself, for even death is hollow and passing swiftly, fading quickly, and consumed away, leaving nothing behind.

Let Us Go You And I

Let us go, you and I,
as that time has passed and then is no more . . .

Let us go, you and I,
through the blind to see what lays ahead . . .

Let us go, you and I,
slipping and leaping along our trail of vision . . .

Let us go, you and I,
to have the courage as we face each new challenge . . .

Let us go, you and I,
with bracelets of love true and pure over the waves . . .

Let us go, you and I,
across the silence to hear our hearts sing each to each . . .

Let us go, you and I,
as we let go heart to heart; let us go you and I . . .

As Sure As Sure Can Be

(Gives Grace To Sing!)

Pure and true hide us in your love,
as sure as sure can be . . .
Only in your abundance
as sure as sure our help stay.
Only in your glow
as sure as sure can we gleam a little ray.

Pure and true hide us in your love,
as sure as sure can be . . .
Only to know your voice as sure as sure is to say.
Only to walk in your path
as sure as sure the very best way.

Pure and true hide us in your love,
as sure as sure can be . . .
Only in your compassion as sure as sure is this day.
Only in your new and living way
as sure as sure does our hope lay.

Pure and true hide us in your love,
as sure as sure can be . . .

Only to become God's finished work
of art do we pray,
As sure as sure can be . . .

In the Face of the Clock

Our faces peer from sleep as movement opens our eyes,
as if suddenly dark canvases are rolled from over us to
reveal what was hidden only moments ago
in the face of the clock.

Each way is free: as the breath is to be breathed to our
lungs and carried to each cell of our body structure.
Each way is free: that was hidden only moments ago
in the face of the clock.

With each tick of the clock something is being birthed and also
something passes beyond moral's understanding. Each
course is not bound and not inhibited. Hidden only moments
ago
in the face of the clock.

Thanksgiving Prayer

BOWED ARE OUR HEADS AS WE
SHARE ONE WITH ANOTHER THIS
THANKSGIVING PRAYER . . .

JUST FOR THIS MOMENT AT THE END
OF THE YEAR, FORGETTING THE ROW,
AND STATION AND RANK . . .

LET US GIVE THANKS TO GOD ABOVE.
THANKSGIVING! THANKSGIVING!
IN EACH OF US HIS DISPLAY OF LOVE.

LET US BE THANKFUL ALL IS PLENTY,
FROM HIM WHO GIVES IT ALL, RICHER,
FULLER OVERFLOWING OUR HEARTS.

"As Leaves Fall"

AS FRAGILE AS THE MOVEMENT OF THE DAYS OF LIFE WHILE HUMANITY REMAINS ON STAGE AS SEASONS COME AND GO.

HUMANITY IS AS A TREE . . . AS LEAVES FALL.

THE SUBJECTING OF HUMANITY . . . FACING DAILY MANY CONCERNS OF WHAT IS AND ROOTED IN THE JOURNEY THAT REMAINS.

AS THE ORDER AND TIMED EVENTS RUSH FORWARD IN WHAT WAS, IS, AND WILL BE, AS ONE IS SO ARE ALL . . . AS LEAVES FALL.

AS HUMANITY IS SUBJECTED IN A STAGED ARRANGEMENT, ONE COMPONENT IN THE COURSE OF ALL PURPOSED PRESENTATION.

HUMANITY IS AS A TREE . . . AS LEAVES FALL.

The Caring Desire That Always Makes A Difference

I want so much to help you and
to let you know I'm always here
for you . . . in this special way that
always makes the difference.

I realize what your going through
is something you must go through
on your own . . . in this special way I
want to tell you, you are not alone.

My heart and my prayers reach out
to you in this special way . . . the
caring desire that always makes the
difference. We can make a difference.

The Silence Garden Of Life

    IF A BUD IN YOUR HAND BLOSSOMED EVERY TIME I REMEMBERED YOU.
    IF A BEE CAME JUST TO GATHER THE NECTAR EVERY TIME I FAVORED YOU.
    IF THE DEW DROPS FAIL ON YOU EVERY TIME I SORROWED FOR YOU.
    IF THE SUN RAYS WARMED YOU EVERY TIME I HELPED YOU.
    THEN YOU COULD KNOW AND REGARD THE SILENCE GARDEN OF LIFE.

Common People Ordinary Things

DESPITE THE FACT WE ARE COMMONLY UNACCEPTABLE AND AT TIMES EVEN DESPAIR OF LIFE, BEING WORN DOWN.

DESPITE THE FACT THAT ORDINARY THINGS ARE NORNAL AND THE ORDER CHARACTERIZED IS EMPLOYED.

ABOVE OUR STRENGHT AND BEYOND OUR ABILITY, BOTH WITHIN AND WITH OUT DAILY GIVEN ALL WE NEED.

EXPERIENCING THE AMAZING GRACE OF GOD, WE LEARN WHAT GOD CAN DO WITH COMMON PEOPLE AND ORDINARY THINGS BY . . . BELIEVING!

Love Remembers

IN THE DEEP YEILDED COMPASSION
    FROM REPENTANCE AND BEING
    BORN AGAIN . . . CAUSING THE
    HEAVEN'S ANGELS TO REJOICE!
IN THE HOPE WHERE POSSIBLES . . .
    ARE PLENTIFUL EVER SOWING
    AS WIND UNDER THE EAGLE'S
    WINGS, THAT IS MADE READY!
IN THE WIDTH OF A TENDER TOUCH
    OF THE MASTER'S HAND WITH
    HIS GRACE . . . BY THE PRECIOUS
    BLOOD OF THE LAMB OF GOD!
IN THE LENGTH OF THE JOY OF
    WORSHIP, PRAISE, AND
    THANKSGIVING . . . HE DIED ON THE
    CROSS! . . . THAT WE MIGHT BE FREE
    AND IN HIS AMAZING GRACE . . .
    HE AROSE! . . . LOVE REMEMBERS!

The Known And The Unknown

WITHIN THE WEB OF THOUGHTS,
TOUCHING ETERITY . . . THAT IS NOT
AFFECTED BY TIME OR MEASURE.
    BY ALLOWING THE PATH OF
THOUGHTS HOW MANY CONCERNS
HAVE OUR KNOWN AND UNKNOWN
THOUGHTS JOINED AS TRAVELERS
IN SPACE AND OUT SIDE OF TIME?
    AS GENERATION TO GENERATION
HOW MANY THOUGHTS HAVE OUR
FAMILY MEMBERS HAVING A COMMON
AIM AND INTEREST . . . MERGED?
SO ARE WE REALLY BECOMING MANY
OR ARE WE ALL BECOMING ONE . . . IN
THE KNOWN AND THE UNKNOWN LONG
AWAITED, WHICH BOTH ARE ENACTED
FOR THE GOOD OF ALL . . . HEAVEN!

The King Is Coming!

THE GREATEST SILENCE AND THE GREATEST STILLNESS WILL HALT ALL EXISTENCE AS NEVER BEFORE. ALL THE EARTH SHALL STARE AT THE HEAVENS IN GREAT WONDERMENT AND GREAT ASTONISHMENT AND WILL MARVEL AT THE AWESOMNESS OF THE HEAVENS GLORY THAT IS DISCLOSED UNIVERSAL . . . AND EVERY KNEE SHALL BOW . . . UNIQUENESS OF THIS MARVEL . . .

THE KING IS COMING!

AWAITED, AS A BRIDEGROOM . . . TO TAKE HIS BRIDE TO THE GLORIOUS MARRIAGE FEAST, PAID FOR BY THE PRECIOUS BLOOD OF THE LAMB, THAT THE WHITE ROBES OF THE BRIDE HAVE BEEN WASHED CLEAN. GENERATIONS OF FAMILIES OF THOSE AWAITING, BUT NEVER RECEIVING THE PROMISED GLORY TO BE DISCLOSED IN GOD'S DUE TIME . . . BELIEVING . . .

THE KING IS COMING!

Get Up And Win The Race

(CARRYING OUR CROSS)
IN A RACE THAT SOMETIMES SEEMS SO HARD TO
RUN. ALL IS GOING WILL AND SUDDENLY WE FALL
FLAT ON OUR FACE. THEN WE HEAR OUR FATHER
SAY,
GET BACK UP AND WIN THE RACE.

SO HERE WE GO AGAIN, TRYING TO CATCH UP, THEN
WE'RE GOING WELL AGAIN AND YES WE FALL FLAT
ON OUR FACE AGAIN. THEN WE HEAR OUR
FATHER SAY
AGAIN, GET UP AND WIN THE RACE. BUT THIS
TIME WHEN WE FAIL
WE COULD NOT GET BACK UP AS FAST
AS WE DID THE FIRST TIME, BECAUSE THE PAIN WE
FELT. THEN WE HEAR THE FATHER SAY AGAIN,
GET UP
AND WIN THE RACE.

SO HERE WE GO AGAIN, TRYING TO PLEASE THE
FATHER, GOING
WELL AGAIN, AND YES WE FALL FLAT
ON OUR FACE AGAIN. THIS TIME WE LOOK UP JUST
IN TIME TO SEE THE WINNER CROSS THE LINE
AHEAD OF US. WE WANT TO GIVE UP,
WHATS THE USE?
THEN THE WINNER SAYS, GET UP AND WIN THE
RACE.

The Divine Grip Of Grace

THE AWESOMENESS OF STANDING BEFORE
THE JUDGE OF THE UNIVERSE . . .

THE FAVORABLENESS OF HIS
AMAZING GRACE WHEN HE SAYS,
" I HAVE CALLED YOU UNTO MYSELF "

THE WONDEROUS WONDER OF IT ALL . . .
HIS AMAZING LOVE DRIVES OUR FAITH.
INSPIRING US AND HELPING US STAND.

THROUGHT IT ALL!

The Holy Divine Grip Of Amazing Grace

WHEREWITH STANDING BEFORE THE
AWESOMENESS OF THE JUDGE OF
THE UNIVERSE; A CONSUMING FIRE.

WHEREBY PASSING THROUGHT HIS
FAVORABLENESS WHEN THE JUDGE OF
THE UNIVERSE SAYS, COME UP HERE.

WHEREFROM THE ANCHOR HOLDS IN
ANTICIPATION AND EXPECTATION;
ALTHOUGH THE SHIP IS HEAVY WORN.

WHEREWITHAL IS MADE READY FOR
THOSE WHO HAVE KEPT THE FAITH AND
WHO'S NAMES ARE WRITTEN IN THE
LAMB'S BOOK OF LIFE.

WHEREAS THOSE BEING FAITHFUL UNTO
DEATH SHALL NOT BE HURT OF THE SECOND
DEATH; THEY SHALL BE GIVEN A CROWN OF
LIFE. SO SHALL WE EVER BE WITH THE LORD!

Basic Endless Endurance (Happy Easter)

A COMMON TREAD THAT
HOLDS EVERYTHING
TOGETHER.

A SUBSTANCE THAT IS THE
ESSENTIAL NEED OF
ANYTHING.

THE INTERMOST CORE
CONTAINING THE SEED
OF CONVICTION.

TO ASSURE THE CERTAINTY
NOT THE END BUT TO MAKE
FIRM A NEW BEGINNING.

The right to life

I don't believe one person or a group . . .
has the right to dictate what is the right for
me. To live and express my life style is my
freedom to decide. (making my own mind up!)

I don't believe one person or a group . . .
has the right to regulate what is the right for
me. To live the scale and degree of my life
is my freedom of choosing. (making my choice!)

I don't believe one person or a group . . .
has the right to waver what is the right for
me. To live the given and due of my life is
my freedom of independence. (through it all!)

The right to life.

Make Us Lord, So Like You

YOUNG AND OLD, LET OUR LIGHT SHINE.
DESIROUS OF THY POWER DIVINE,
NOT ASHAMED TO OPENLY LIVE SHINING,
AND THROWING OUT THE LIFELINE.

A SINGLE LIGHT THAT PROVIDES HOPE
AND ENCOURAGEMENT; ILLUSTRATING OUR
SPIRITUAL RESPONSIBILITY IN THE DARKEST
NIGHT, TO A FAILING DYING WORLD.

THAT WE MIGHT BE PREPARED, TO STAND
STRONG, LET OUR LIGHT SO SHINE THAT
EVERYONE IN THE HOUSE HAS LIGHT. AS
A LIGHT THAT COULD NOT BE HIDDEN.

THAT OUR INFLUENCE CONTINUALLY BE
OBVIOUS, THAT WE ARE FOLLOWING ONE
WHO COULD NOT BE HIDDEN.
MAKE US LORD, SO LIKE YOU.

Forever Grateful

The joy of being forgiven
safe in the arms of JESUS!

The power of His precious
blood through it all!

The effectiveness of His
compassion new every day!

The unspeakable gift renown
beginning to end fullness!

Make Available

JESUS . . . OUR LIVING HOPE.

BECAUSE HIS NAME IS HOLY . . .
BECAUSE OF WHO HE IS . . .
BECAUSE OF ALL HE HAS
WONDEROUSLY PROVIDED . . .
BECAUSE HE IS DAILY THERE
TO GUIDE AND PROTECT . . .
BECAUSE HE AND HE ALONE
IS ABLE TO SATISFY . . .
BECAUSE HE HAS ALL POWER
HIS VICTORY IS COMPLETE . . .
BECAUSE HE IS WORTHY OF
CREATION ENDLESS PRAISE . . .
BECAUSE JESUS GAVE WHAT
ONLY HE COULD GIVE . . .
. . . HIMSELF . . .
(THERE IS NO OTHER)
BECAUSE LIFE'S JOY MADE
AVAILABLE UNTO HIM TODAY
IS AVAILABLE TO WHOSOEVER . . .
BECAUSE ALL ARE COMPLETE
HIM IN ALL AND ALL IN HIM.

Ascribe Unto The Lord

HELP US LORD . . . WHEN WE DON'T KNOW WHAT TO DO.

HELP US LORD . . . WHEN WE KNOW WHAT TO DO, BUT WE DON'T WANT TO DO IT.

HELP US LORD . . . MOST OF ALL NOT TO CLING TIGHTLY TO WHAT DISPLEASES YOU.

HELP US LORD . . . DAILY TO SEEK THY SWEET WISDOM TO GUIDE AND PROTECT US.

HELP US LORD . . . STAY CLOSE TO OUR SIDE BOTH IN GOOD TIMES AND TIMES OF SORROW.

Before We Be No More

OUR DAYS ARE FEW
MANY ARE THE SNARES
BEFORE WE BE NO MORE.
OUR LIFES ARE FRAGILE
MANY ARE THE TEARS
BEFORE WE BE NO MORE.
OUR CONCERNS ARE GREAT
MANY ARE THE DEBATES
BEFORE WE BE NO MORE.
OUR VALUES ARE TESTED
MANY ARE THE TRIALS
BEFORE WE BE NO MORE.
OUR COMFORTS ARE DIVINE
MANY ARE THE SHADOWS
BEFORE WE BE NO MORE.

A Personal Choice

We don't need to scarch
to find our way.

We need only The Good
Shepherd to lead us daily.

A Personal Choice.

(No matter what He is
Greater and He is not
finished with us yet.)

And in everything give
thanks unto the LORD!

We will yet Praise The
LORD for His Wonderous
Wonderful Wonders.

PRAISE THE LORD!

WE DRAW FROM

THE NOURISHMENT

AND SURE SUPPORT

EACH DAY

WE TAKE A MOMENT

WITH THE LORD.

Motive More Meaningful

WE ARE SPECIAL IN A SPECIAL WAY
A DETAILED ACCOUNT HAS BEEN PUT
FOREVER IN OUR HEARTS AND MINDS.

WE ARE SPECIAL IN A SPECIAL WAY
A IDENTICAL COPY FOREVER BOTH
EXISTING AND GROWING BENEFITS.

WE ARE SPECIAL IN A SPECIAL WAY
A ADVANTAGEOUS INVOLVEMENT MORE
MEANINGFUL THAN OURSELVES.

WE ARE SPECIAL IN A SPECIAL WAY
A PARTICULAR PEOPLE SPECIFICALLY
THE WORKMANSHIP FROM START TO
FINISH GOD'S OWN WORK OF ART.

Taste the air

Taste the air
all is newness.

Taste the air
all is currentness.

Taste the air
all is oneness.

Taste the air
all is all.

"GREAT IS THY FAITHFULNESS!"
LAM. 3:20-26 Ö JOHN 1:29Ö ISA. 55:11

NOTHING BUT THE BLOOD OF

JESUS THE LAMB OF GOD!

THANKSGIVING PRAISE!

Only One Answer

IF IT REQUIRED A SPECIFIC KNOWLEDGE
GOD WOULD HAVE PROVIDED A PROCESS
OF SCHOOLING.

IF IT REQUIRED A SPECIFIC IMPROVEMENT
TO REPAIR SOME PARTICULAR PURPOSE
GOD WOULD HAVE PROVIDED AN EXPERT.

IF IT REQUIRED A SPECIFIC CONDITION
TO REMEDY THE EXCEPTIONAL REPROACH
GOD WOULD HAVE PROVIDED THE EVENT.

AT THE CROSS GOD PROVIDED GOOD WILL
GRACE WITH JESUS UNTO REMORSE OF SIN
PROCESS OF A REPENTANT YIELDED HEART.
(HOLINESS BEATIFIES HIS HOUSE FOREVER.)
JESUS CLOTHED WITH HIS MAJESTY ON HIGH
SETTING AT THE RIGHT HAND OF HIS FATHER
THAT WE MAY DEPART FROM HELL BENEATH.

CASTING OUR CARES UPON OUR SAVIOUR.
JESUS ALONE CAN SATISFY OUR DEEPEST
LONGING AND HE HEARS OUR HEART'S CRY.

May The Word Of God Bless Us

Both Fully God And Fully Man
This Tabernacle Is Complete.

Both Justful And Trueful
This Valuation Is Final.

Both Now And Forever
This Consolation Is Sure.

Man Must Live By This Word
To Find Sufficient Point To Life.

JESUS Came And HE Is Risen!

(JESUS Came And He Is Risen, Because
What We Really Needed Was A SAVIOUR.)

From The Heavens To The Earth
JESUS CAME To Manifest Power.

From Earth To The Rugged Cross
JESUS CAME To Pay Our Pardon.

From The Cross To The Grave
JESUS CAME To Win The Victory.

From The Grave To The Heavens
JESUS CAME AND HE IS RISEN!

(From Death, Hell, And The Grave
JESUS Manifested Power Over All.)

BECAUSE JESUS LIVES, And Is Lifted
Up To Draw Us From The Old Dying
Way To The NEW LIVING WAY!

Luke 10:20 JUBILEE!

The Heavens Shall Open Removing The Vail
Permanently As The Holy One Of Israel Is
Announced Proclaiming JESUS' Presence.

Unto The Children Of Israel Which Cannot
Be Numbered Nor Measured It Shall Be Said
To Them You Are The Sons Of The LIVING GOD.

And Everyone That Shall Be Known As The
Redeemed There Names Shall Be Found Written
In Heaven Nothing Shall By Any Means Hurt Them.

Embracing HIS Promises Lest The Cross Be Of
No Result If We Shall Glory Let Us Glory In
The Cross And Comfort One Another.

We Unto Jesus, Jesus Unto His Father

Our Relationship Best Of All Means Is
God's Amazing Grace Unto Us.

Unto The Uttermost Made Whole With His
Beloved Favor Blest Of The Cross.

The Blessed Consecration Applied Once
By A Holy Vow Of A Strong Affection.

At The Time Chosen By God Are All Things
Of What He Has Compassionately Commanded.

Walk Before God

That We Walk In Newness Of Life Wherein
Not As Fools But As Wise Circumspectly.
Those Who Honor God Will He Honor.

That We Walk In Confident Belief Wherein
Not As Defeated But As Blessed Victorious.
Those Who Honor God Will He Honor.

That We Walk Enjoined Bodily In Christ Wherein
Not As Unrestrained But As Children Of Light.
Those Who Honor God Will He Honor.

Shine! Shine! Shine!

The LORD of Lords is coming!
Darkness withdraws abruptly!

The KING of Kings is coming!
Flavorless carnality vanishes!

Repent! The LORD of Lords! Is
fully victorious in conflict!

Repent! The KING of Kings!
Triumphant knowing no defeat!

Faces of our hearts (OUR GLORIOUS)

Faces Of Our Hearts Having Many Prayers Within.
THE HOLY ONE is Forever More Making Intercession.
Honor Be The Glory Of THE LORD In HIS Place!

Faces Of Our Hearts Having Many Eyes Within.
THE HOLY ONE is Continually Magnified Therein.
Worthy Be The Glory Of THE LORD in HIS Place!

Faces Of Our Hearts Having Many Ears Within.
THE HOLY ONE is Gladly Perceived Without Ceasing.
Worship Be The Glory Of THE LORD in HIS Place!

Faces Of Our Hearts Having Many Voices Within.
THE HOLY ONE is Endless Praise Of Rejoicing Jubilee.
Blessed Be The Glory Of THE LORD in HIS Place!

The Gospel

JESUS could have called the angels in heaven
to go into all the earth with THE GOSPEL.

JESUS could have come only to the religious
to go into all the earth with THE GOSPEL.

JESUS could have come only to the wise
to go into all the earth with THE GOSPEL.

JESUS instead came to fishermen and used
simple parables to go into all the earth.

Against the odds

America resolved the result and prayer no
longer has a deeply rooted place in public.

America resolved the result and refrains no
longer has a deeply rooted place in public.

Trash bags and trash bags all heaped up in
piles of abortions leaving no chance for denial.

Body bags and body bags all heaped up in
piles of overdosed leaving no chance for denial.

How much more of this evil corrupted intrusion
and harmfully perverted practices will GOD take?

Deliberate The Origin And Design Of A Pearl

The unmerited favor granted to tiny grains of sand and it's poetic composition as a hourglass measures time.

The although process as a journey daily requirements of specify details benefits expenses have been met.

The unfolding presentations itself steady poetic insight granting blessing to the chosen create cause to occur.

The unbroken degree poetry of a high order employed unit of latitude and longitude of a great complete circle.

Mastering the notes

Mastering the notes . . .
As the notes themselves skillfully
control each master-stroke.

Mastering the notes . . .
As the notes themselves prefix
address each master key.

Mastering the notes . . .
As the notes themselves make
expertly bold each mastery.

Mastering the notes . . .
As the notes themselves beckon
unto the poet's mastership.

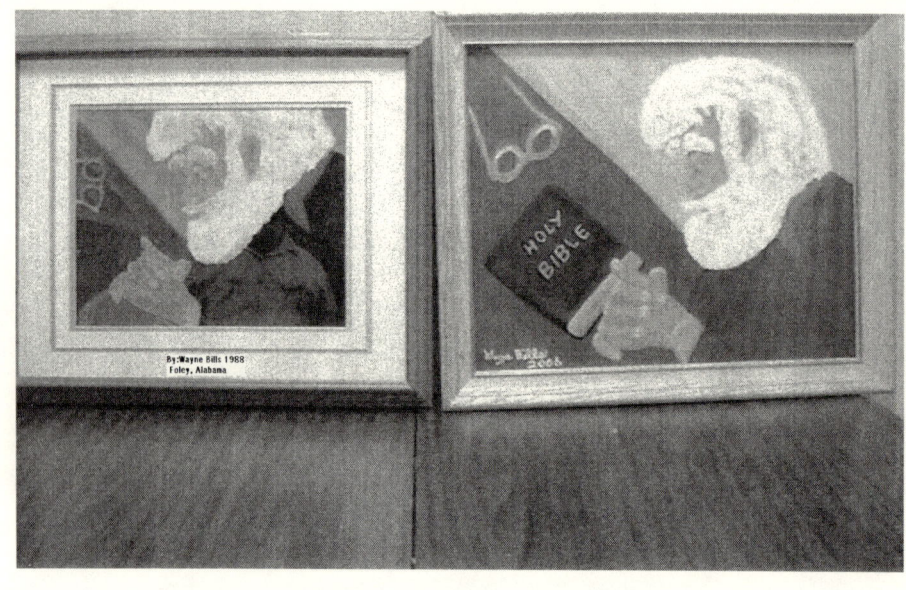

Keep praying

OVER THE YEARS . . .
WE HAVE HAD MANY
PRAYERS WE HAVE
PRAYED FOR OTHERS.
KEEP PRAYING!

OVER THE YEARS . . .
WE HAVE HAD MANY
PRAYERS PRAYED
BY OTHERS FOR US.
KEEP PRAYING!

Numbering Our Days

Each day when it has passed granting and
            permitting both
            wisdom and refuge rested on
inner fixed limits or extent
            of in time by Divine means
and favorable support of in time.

            As in the morning they are
like grass which grow-up. Each
            day we open our eyes in our
dwelling and rise-up our eyes to
            established length of our
days wherein is wisdom and refuge.

            A fool does not understand
this therefore he can not apply
            his heart unto wisdom.
Remember how short our day time is!
            In the name of Our LORD
have we daily set-up our banners.

No Greater Love

Sufficient is secured by manifold copy . . .
A specific kind ability requirement
adequate with as much as needed.

Acceptance is binded by affixed root . . .
A creative inspiration impulse that
drives the urging results until finished.

Grace is effortless unmerited favor . . .
A Divine Love freely rendered by
One who need not do so. *Paid in full.*

Riches
(Wisdom From Above)

It is one's heart that reveals where one's
pleasures therein are gladly received as a loyal
companionship of compassion to take hold in.

It is one's heart in a favorable and correct
conduct therein where ones well-regulated life
conveys as well as in held one day at a time.

It is one's heart that makes one prosperous . . .
To Whom and to what one's heart therein stand.
TO WALK THE WALK, not just talk the talk.

Bright Morning Star

Bright morning star is becoming more
apparent as the drawing of a new day
arises far and wide with opened arms.
O that man would praise THE LORD.

Although existing age to age yet still
fashionable being the first and only
to come quick and brightly into view.
O that man would praise THE LORD.

In intimate unlimited harmony and an
obvious earnest perceptible agreement
placed firmly a special predestination.
O that man would praise THE LORD.

Purchased . . . Made Closer To Him
(Touching Jesus Is All That Matters)

To put behind yesterday to earnestly resume Today.
To relinquish the waste to obeying what is to adjust.
To depart the entangled to yield meekly to find rest.
To leave the worthless to hold fast to the necessary.

To flee the corruption to seek to walk respectability.
To remedy the enfeebled to clutch to a high calling.
To put aside the chains to welcoming the Comforter.
To refusing the fraud ways to a new and living way.

To temperance to the truth Christ has made all free.
To seal all of He redeemed by His precious blood.
To not be guilty before Him to awake to eternal life.
To His purchased possession . . . made closer to Him.

Valley Of Dreams
(Keeping The Spark)

At the beginning and finish of each page of our existence
the breathe is a gulp of air taken in to use up and let out.
The vigorous action of life survival effort that is required.
Through it all . . . correspondingly God is there in believing.

We only see in our mind's eye sparking respite life's way.
As in valentines on Valentine Day the card says Be Mine.
Thus we set up our banners to make our hearts known.
Through it all . . . correspondingly God is there in believing.

As we act in return or in answer sustaining our pledges.
As in symbolizing where resilient grace is readily furnish.
Thus taking heart in a better pleasing likeness we accept.
Through it all . . . correspondingly God is there in believing.

Bidden to Come

To offer the utmost purpose of intentions and a
arrangement of magnificence splendor in array.
Utterly devoid bid of any margins of inaccuracy.
Accompanying . . . The marriage feast of THE LAMB.

In grand audience among the rejoicing number present.
And part in the awe wondrous wonderful wonder of it all.
The fullness of joy shining in the face of our Redeemer.
Accompanying . . . The marriage feast of THE LAMB.

And in humble solemn adoration thanksgiving praise and pure
dedicated affectionate worship. Worthy is the LAMB!
Fully consecrated and grand companionship rewarded bliss.
All in awe found written in awesome LAMB's Book Of Life.
Accompanying . . . The marriage feast of THE LAMB.

To My Children *(I Wish You Love)*

Dare I remember the times and voices of what
only seems like yesterday I hear the laugher I
see the tears the sun coming and going down.
Pressed in the glow and pushed in the woe.
Dare I gaze upon the memories the pain is to
great to bare recalling past experiences held
as preserved pleasant and events of account.
Pressed in the glow and pushed in the woe.
Dare I keep in mind care forlorn children are
special measures the hurt is enormous to recall
damage the times and voices of yore yet again.
Pressed in the glow and pushed in the woe.
I pray never wonder if I . . . cared . . . I always . . . care.
I trust you know . . . to remember . . . upsets me so.

I Can Feel You My Lord Breathing

(Welcome HOLY SPIRIT . . . YEA! FILL US AGAIN)

A single moment of movement to regain the
subjective impacted respiration means of life.
      I can feel YOU MY LORD breathing.

I close my eyes and breathe in only through
my nose I can perceive a sensation hurry in.
      I can feel YOU MY LORD breathing.

As a encoded course of action repeated over
and over I can be aware of a lively perception.
      I can feel YOU MY LORD breathing.

In The Hands Of Our Lord

Sometimes we can't understand why
this life beats us up so bad and neither
know we what to do.

Oh! sometimes we grow so dishearten
and we wonder if the sun will ever shine
again and neither know we what to do.

But by Faith our times are in the hands
of our Lord. So, my dear friend don't grief
too long, but raise your head and smile.

In the hands of our Lord keep rejoicing
with me, my dear friend where THE
LAMB OF GOD is the light thereof.

Jesus . . . is Love In Any Language

The breadth, The length,, The depth, The height . . . Is firmly settled faith here inside this Seed.

This rootage of grace Seed, sufficient with better revelation, better hope, better priesthood,
better covenant, better promises, better sacrifice, better country, and better resurrection.

We are not our own seed; we are a fellowship hid in God, according to the eternal purpose
which God purposed in Christ JESUS our Lord. That Christ may dwell in our hearts by faith.

We whom pertaining to this Seed are as many as sands and stars can number cause HIS
compassions fail not they are new every morning. A sure rootage flowing with living water

We are more than conquerors, sealed in HIS SPIRIT, washed white as snow in HIS precious
blood. And there is daily reaffirmed blessed assurance in this Seed, cause *'GOD SO LOVED!!'*

The Sinner's Prayer

JESUS . . . NEVER BECOMES WEARY WITH THEM
THAT HAVE A BROKEN HEART NOR THOSE OF
US, WHO UPON HIM CAST . . . OUR EVERY CARE.

WHEN WE REPENT WITH WEEPING AND PRAY . . .
YIELDING OUR TRIED AND TORN HEARTS, FOR
WE KNOW WHEN SORROWS HAVE VISITED US.

HE WAS ACQUAINTED WITH GRIEF. A MAN OF
SORROWS, AND EVEN FASTEN TO A CROSS.
MEEKLY, HE REWARDS THE SINNER'S PRAY.

WE ACCEPT FAITH, HIS LOVE AND WORDS ARE
TRUE, JESUS REDEEMED US WITH HIS BLOOD.
IN BELIEVING WE KNOW, AND ARE PERSUADED.

ONLY JESUS CAN HEAR OUR HEART'S CRY.
AND HE CAN SATISFY OUR DEEPEST DESIRE.
ONLY JESUS IS ABLE TO CLEANSE OUR SINS.

Trip Of My Life Time

(I Walked!! . . . Where . . . JESUS Walked!!)

ISRAEL . . . IN ONE WORD, INCOMPREHENSIBLE!!

Oceans and oceans of people, like inflowing currents that could sweep us away if we don't keep our eyes on our guide . . . He says COME!

COME, it's a cleansing walk, a narrow path to walk where JESUS walked. His blessing is there toward the uttermost . . . A great gain to COME!

COME, it's a conviction . . . redeemed purchased from our sins, back to His righteousness base to anew . . . anchored and assuredness to COME!

COME, it's a submissive obedient, acceptance pertaining to authority, as a much better hope awaited . . . Israel's King and Kingdom to COME!

COME, COME TO ISRAEL!! <u>(YOU"LL NEVER BE THE SAME!!)</u>

My Faith Defines Who I Am . . .

I GOT TO BE WHO I AM . . .
TO BE WHO I AM!!

NOT TO MAKE YOU HAPPY . . .
BUT TO MAKE . . . MYSELF HAPPY!!

Face Down Again

THE AGONY AHEAD—DEATH TERRIFIES US. AND
EVEN TRYING TO FACE LIFE'S THREATENING
SORROW IS AGONY TO THE LAST GASPING
FOR THE
LAST MOUTHFUL OF AIR—BEFORE WE BE NO
MORE.

AS MORALS THE STEEP CLIMB BEFORE US, SEEMS
TO CONTINUOUSLY CAUSE GRIEF AND SUFFERING.
AND WE ALL HAVE OUR DISTRESS, OLD SCARS AND
OUR PAINFUL NEW WOUNDS. FACE DOWN AGAIN.

FROM LOW IN THE DUST AND FROM THE GROUND
ECHO SHALL OUR WHISPER BE HEARD?
TODAY HELP
US LORD!!—IN OUR WEAKNESS IS THINE
STRENGTH.
CONSENCRATED IN JESUS'
BLOOD—FOREVERMORE!

Jesus Saves!!!

JESUS does extraordinary things to satisfy the value of a single soul.
JESUS left heaven's glory to reach high and low and far and wide.
JESUS did not minimize even a young child who desired to come.
JESUS never underestimated or lost sight of the value of one soul.

JESUS does extraordinary things to satisfy the value of a single soul.
JESUS had a major conversation with one Samaria woman at a well.
JESUS called one thrilled man to come down from a sycamore tree.
JESUS never underestimated or lost sight of the value of one soul.

JESUS found great faith a centurion who said, speak the word only.
JESUS said someone touched me, and said her faith made her whole.
JESUS in time of sorrow restored life to lamenting woman's dead son.
JESUS never underestimated or lost sight of the value of one soul.

Widen Our Vision

(JOHN 3:16)

JESUS WIDEN OUR VISION: THAT THE SENSATION AND
EXCITEMENT OF THY COMPASSION IS ROUND ABOUT US.
OPEN OUR EYES THAT WE MIGHT NOT ONLY SEE BUT
RECOGNIZE OUR WIDEN VISION, BEAUTY OF HOLINESS.

JESUS WIDEN OUR VISION: TO VIEW NOT STRANGERS AND
UNLOVED PEOPLE BUT PEOPLE HAVING NEEDS OF AS WE.
OPEN OUR EYES THAT WE MIGHT NOT ONLY SEE BUT
RECOGNIZE OUR WIDEN VISION, OURSELVES SO LOVED..

JESUS WIDEN OUR VISION: THAT WE LOOK NOT AT THE
WORLD WITH UNSEEING EYES AS THE TIME DRAWS NEAR..
OPEN THERE EYES THAT THEY MIGHT NOT ONLY SEE BUT
RECOGNIZE AS US. THE PERFECT GIFT OF GOD . . . IS THEE.

Love His Salvation

We have an promised incorruptible
inheritance if
we hold fast the confidence and
the rejoicing of
the hope firm unto the end. He
upholding all things
by the word of His power, when He
purged our sins.

Purchased possession unto
Salvation, sealed with
that HOLY SPIRIT of
promise, which is the earnest
of our inheritance unto
redemption . . . that we have
received the adoption of sons
confirmed in our hearts.

Whereby JESUS shall change our
vile body, that it
may be fashioned like unto His
glorious body, that
we who's names are in the book of
life, and love His
salvation say continually, Let God
Be Magnified!!!

Happy 2008 ISRAEL Sixtieth Up To: Jerusalem!
(The White Stone)

THE WHITE STONE, JERUSALEM'S Icon!!!
As A Matter Of Fact: It Is Against The Law
To Use Any Other Color Stone In The Finish
Construction Of Any Building In JERUSALEM.

When The Light Shines Upon JERUSALEM,
THE WHITE STONE Icon In Representation Of
The Awesomeness Beauty Of Holiness Forms
An Inspiring Awe Golden Yellow Color Of Purity.

Moving The Mountain

On our knees is where we move the mountain, by praying JESUS take my eyes off myself and let me see that I can't move this mountain, but by Faith.

Ourselves the mountain, that Faith must settle in a new place. JESUS changing ourself, from guilty to forgiven, By the Power Of His Awesome Spoken Word.

Looking Unto JESUS, we are His join heirs, He is not finish with you and I yet, but we are His workmanship, praying always with all prayer and supplication in The Spirit.

Shining Shield! And Shining Sword!

(GREAT IS THY FAITHFULNESS!)

O, SHINING LAMB OF CALVARY SAVIOUR AWE DIVINE!
LET US IN EARNEST FROM THIS DAY WHOLLY BE THINE!
THINE HEART IS TOUCHED WITH OUR PAINS AND TEARS
O, OUR BANNERS THAT WE MIGHT LEAVE THEM THERE.

O, SHINING LAMB OF CALVARY SAVIOUR AWE DIVINE!
LET US NOT FAIL BUT FROM THIS DAY WHOLLY BE THINE!
HEAR US WHEN OUR HEARTS CRY UNTO THEE THOUGH
ALL ELSE FAILS WHEN SHAKEN. LET US NOT BE SHAKEN.

O, SHINING LAMB OF CALVARY SAVIOUR AWE DIVINE!
LET OUR REVERENCE FROM THIS DAY WHOLLY BE THINE!
DROPS Of MERCIES AROUND US SHOWERS OUR NEEDS,
O, SHOWERS OF BLESSINGS, JESUS FILLS OUR CUPS.

ISRAEL, Holy Ground

O, ISRAEL does my heart and pen rejoice to write of Thee!
O, ISRAEL, THE HOLY LAND O, how AWESOME the experience!
O, ISRAEL, I will always embrace, The Trip Of My Life Time.
O, ISRAEL, God's own selected and desired choice, PEACE!!!
O, ISRAEL Does My Heart And Pen Rejoice To Write Of Thee!!!

Feeling Jesus' Warmth!!!

TO LOVE AND BE LOVED John 3:16
(FEEL JESUS WARMTH!!!)

To Love And Be Loved A Personal Divine Given Compassion.
The Strongest Power That Travels Furthest And Fastest.
The Greatest Sacred Extent; Conveying Endlessly HIS Amazing Grace.

To Love And Be Loved A Personal Divine Given Compassion . . .
ABIDING IN JESUS COMPASSION . . . FEELING JESUS WARMTH!!!
Awesomely daily enriching—THE BLOOD BOUGHT—THE REDEEMED.

Forgiveness!!!

I'M BLOOD BOUGHT!!!
PRECIOUS HOLY LAMB OF CALVARY (GAL. 6:14)
("'THE WAY OF THE CROSS'")

O, Shining LAMB OF CALVARY Savior Awe Divine! . . . Our Holy Rock Of Ages!
Via Dolorosa! Nothing Is Able To Disunite (Undo) The Blood Redeemed Ones!
Rejoicing!!! Giving Thanks Always In The Precious Name Of JESUS!!!
The Everlasting Covenant Of God's Divine Token Given
Us Unto Salvation, Making The Way Straight And Narrow Before Our Face.
Desiring JESUS, Come Into Our Hearts Forevermore. Heart To Heart !!!
May We, FEELING JESUS WARMTH AGAIN!!! With Yielded Hearts From This Day
Wholly Be Thine, And In Joy Of Thy Precious Name We Have Set Up Our Banners.
O, Shining LAMB OF CALVARY Savior Awe Divine! . . . Our Holy Rock Of Ages!
Via Dolorosa! Nothing Is Able To Disunite (Undo) The Blood Redeemed Ones!
Rejoicing!!! Giving Thanks Always In The Precious Name Of JESUS!!!
Though All That Be Found Without Faith Shall No Longer
Continue, When All Nations Are Shaken In The Day Of

The LORD, Need fully, Our Prayers We Direct Unto Thee. FEELING JESUS
WARMTH!!! May We Find Comfort As . . . Thy Holy Spirit Helps Us Remain?
Restoring Us Again, With . . . The Endless Joy Of Thy Salvation. Leading Us In The
Pathway Of Righteousness! Children Of The KING!
O, Shining LAMB OF CALVARY Savior Awe Divine! . . . Our Holy Rock Of Ages!
Via Dolorosa! Nothing Is Able To Disunite (Undo) The Blood Redeemed Ones!
Rejoicing!!! Giving Thanks Always In The Precious Name Of JESUS!!!
With Drops Of Mercies Compass Us, And Shower Our Needs. Heart To Heart !!!
May We In All Earnest Virtues, FEELING JESUS WARMTH AGAIN!!! From This
Day Wholly Be Thine. Lifting . . . Thy Glory And Praise With Joyful Rejoicing,
Forevermore. No Other Source Of Sacrifice Do We Know! (I'M SO THANKFUL,
FOR JESUS PRECIOUS REDEEMING BLOOD THAT COVERS ME . . .
TILL THERE BE NO MORE SIN.) Nothing But The Precious Redeeming
Blood Of JESUS, That Washes Us . . . Whiter Than Snow!!! ALLELUIA!!!

Godhearted Clothed Multitude
HEB. 12:1, 2

(Blessed Are The Pure In Heart.) THE DIVINE AWESOME GRANDEUR OF GOD!!!

(Note: LIVING BY ... FAITH!!! FEELING JESUS WARMTH!!! Through It All. It's Been Mercy All The Way. My Heavenly Father, I Bow Down I'm Forever Grateful!!!)

Godhearted, Born Again, Joyful Hearts Ringing In Pure Worship And Pure Praise!
Thanksgiving! Responding To The Situation Wisely As Clothed Obedience
Children, Feeling JESUS Warmth!!! With Their Names Written In The LAMB'S
Book Of Life! Faith Desiring And Awaiting God's Affirmative Appointed Time Be
Fully Accomplished, Divine Completeness In His Consecrated Work, Faith In
Christ Made Perfect.

Looking Unto JESUS, The Divine Beauty Of Holiness! Having Good Will Toward
Men, And Above All, Recall The Godhearted Who Are Being Persecuted And
Suffering For Their Faithful Position Within The Everlasting Gospel. Feeling

JESUS Warmth!!! Passionately! JESUS Cleansing A Peculiar People Unto
Himself. In All Kinds Of Prayers, Significantly, The Grace Of God Unto
Salvation Has Appeared Unto Men!

Faith . . . Was, Is, And Shall Be Settled Evermore Through And In CHRIST JESUS,
Unto Salvation! Shining Each Day Ever So Brighter, Feeling JESUS Warmth!!! The
Victor's Promised Triumph, Glorious Kingdom Of JESUS! As Countless Unite In
The Singing. Feeling JESUS Warmth!!! 'Worthy Is The Lamb of God!'
Hosanna! Shouts Unto JESUS! HIS Precious Blood Saving Power Redeemed Us
Free Indeed To God! Washes Us Whiter Than Snow!

O, That Awesome Place . . . Where JESUS Presence Fills Every Song!!! And The
Joy, Gladness Praises, And Worship Goes On And On And On Forevermore. As
The Godhearted Clothed Multitude Fill The Universe With Sovereignty Shouts
And Songs Of The Blood Redeemed Freedom. When The Desire Cometh It Is A
Tree Of Life With Fruits Of Righteousness Yielding Everlasting Fruit. And There
Shall Be No More Cruse. As The Godhearted Clothed Multitude See JESUS Face.

Our Faith In JESUS Still Gentle Voice
I Pet. 5:6,7; 2 COR. 12:9

(LIVING BY . . . FAITH!!! FEELING HIS WARMTH!!! IT'S BEEN MERCY ALL THE WAY!!!
Luke 24:32 MY HEAVENLY FATHER, I Humbly Bow Down. Nothing Can Undo
What . . . JESUS PRECIOUS REDEEMING BLOOD Has Done For Me. THANKSGIVING)

When I Feel Loyalty Crushing Temptation Trials, And Harmful Corrupting Sin From
Disgraceful Sources Bearing Down Upon My Heart In The Storms Of Life That
Seems To Blow Me Off My Feet. JESUS, Sustain Me By Your Word, I Will Be Still; I
Want To Pay Attention Unto You, With All My Heart, On A Daily Basis! LIVING BY . . .
FAITH!!! FEELING JESUS WARMTH!!! Through It All, I've Learn To Trust IN JESUS,

When I Feel Deceitfully Affected By Pretend, Counterfeit And Misleading
Appearances, From Deceitfulness Sources, Bearing Down Upon My Heart In The
Storms Of Life That Seems To Blow Me Off My Feet. JESUS, Sustain Me By Your
Word. I Will Be Still; I Want To Listen To You, With All My Heart, On A Daily Basis!

LIVING BY . . . FAITH!!! FEELING JESUS WARMTH!!! Through it All, JESUS Rescue Me.

When I Feel Misery With Bewilderment, That Urges Me To Abandon Calm
Excellent Virtue's Heart-set. From Panic Sources, When Life Becomes To Much To
Handle, Bearing Down On My Heart In The Storms Of Life That Seems To Blow Me
Off My Feet. JESUS, Sustain Me By Your Word. I Will Be Still; JESUS Prop Me Up On
My Leaning Side. I Want To Hear Your Still Gentle Voice!, With All My Heart, On A
Daily Basis! Living By . . . Faith!!! FEELING JESUS WARMTH!!! Through It All, All Joy.

Heb. 12:2 I'm In The Blood!!! ALLELUIA! ALLELUIA!
(I AM MY BELOVED! AND MY BELOVED IS MINE! ALLELUIA THANKSGIVING
Whatever JESUS Tells Me To Do . . . I Want To Do It, With All My Heart, On A Daily
Basis! Living By . . . Faith!!! FEELING HIS WARMTH!!! THY WILL BE DONE, May I Daily
Hid Myself In Thee!!! PS. 32:7 MY HEAVENLY FATHER, I Humbly Bow Down.
Nothing Can Undo What . . . JESUS PRECIOUS REDEEMING BLOOD Has Done For

Me. ALLELUIA THANKSGIVING . . . WAIT UPON THE LORD, PRAISE JESUS. JESUS
WILL DAILY TAKE CARE OF ME. GREAT IS THY FAITHFULNESS!!! Through it all, I count it ALL JOY, And I'm So Grateful JESUS Has Said, "IT IS FINISHED" And Then
Came The Morning . . . The Angel Rolled The Stone Away!!! HE IS RISEN!!! Amen)

ISRAEL! The Holy Ground!
PS. 122

O, Israel . . .
A Land, A People, A Promise, A Blessing.
SHALOM / PEACE!
Does My Heart And Pen . . . REJOICE!
To Write Of Thee!

O, Israel . . .
To Walk . . . Where . . . JESUS Walked!
How Awesome, My First-Hand Experience!
Priceless, And Merry Are My Reminders!

O, Israel . . .
I Will Always Embrace My Pilgrimage!
The Awesomeness! Hold The Good!
Greatly Pleasing, Trip Of My Life Time!

O, Israel . . .
ALMIGHTY GOD'S Own Selected Choice!
He has Desired Thee In All His Wisdom!
God's Wisdom Who Dare Go Against Israel ?

O, Israel . . .
A Land, A People, A Promise! A Blessing.
SHALOM / PEACE!
Does My Heart And Pen . . . REJOICE!
To Write Of Thee!

Feeling Jesus Warmth!!!
Luke 24:32
Joy In The Lord Jesus Always!

As Sure As Sure Can Be! JESUS Alone Can Restore To Health The Heart's Countenances!
JESUS Alone Convincingly Is Capable Of Making Any Vicious Circumstance Quickly Vanish!
Fastened Securely And Fixed Firmly In Place; We Have A Inheritance Incorruptible In Christ!
(Greater things are yet to come!!! GREATER THINGS ARE YET TO BE DONE!!!)
ALLEIUIA! . . . No Greater Feeling Then FEELING JESUS WARMTH!!! In Our Hearts Again!!! HEART TO HEART!!!

How Many Times Have We Not Known What We Should Do? How Many Times Have We
Been Uncertain, With Lack Of Conviction? How Often Have We Been Where We Should
Not Be? And How Often Have We Not Been Where We Should Be? Yet Through It All!
ALLELUIA! . . . No Greater Feeling Then FEELING JESUS WARMTH!!! In Our Hearts Again!!! HEART TO HEART!!!

Pouring In The Oil And Wine; Opening The Prison Doors; Saying Touch Not My Anointed!!!

We Have Set-up Our Banners In The Precious Name Of JESUS! Wait Upon The LORD!!!

HE Will Hear Us From HIS HOLY HEAVEN With The Saving Strength Of HIS Right Hand!!!

ALLELUIA! . . . No Greater Feeling Then FEELING JESUS WARMTH!!! In Our Hearts Again!!! HEART TO HEART!!!

THANKSGIVING PRAISE AND WORSHIP UNTO THE LAMB OF GOD HIS BLOOD HAS

MADE US . . . HIS PURCHASED POSSESSION!!!. THAT WE MIGHT DAILY EARNESTLY BE

RESPONSTIVE AND JOYFULLY ACQAINTED WITH ALL ETERNITY HE HAS SET BEFORE

US!!! That We Might Escaped The Corruption Of Lust; Putting Away The Filth Of The Flesh

Being Quickened And Sealed In HIS Holy Spirit! By The Power Of JESUS PRECIOUS

BLOOD!!! That We Might Be Partakers Of HIS DIVINE NATURE!!! LET THE REDEEMED SAY

SO!!! FEELING JESUS WARMTH!!! In Our Hearts Again!!! HEART TO HEART!!! ALLELUIA!!! ALLELUIA!!!ALLELUIA!!!

Via Dolorosa!!!
Isaiah 53

Down A Very Narrow Passage . . . My Introspects
With A Great Expanse Of Those Who Have Come
Before Me And Those Who Will Come After Me.
THE STREET THE HOLY LAMB OF GOD WALKED!!!

This Extraordinary Occasion . . . Brings Immediately
A boundless Sequence Of Powerful Passions!!!
Even The Meanings Of Passing Times Have Not
Changed These Divine Affixed Evident Signatures.
ALLELUIA!!! ALLELUIA!!! ALLELUIA!!!
NOTHING BUT THE PRECIOUS BLOOD OF JESUS!!!

Hand Grafted In At The Seams
Matt. 6:33

At The Seams Where Life Creativity Is Strongest And Surely Is Guaranteed. Trustworthiness Is to be found In Each Knitted Together
Stitch All Along Their Edges Where Yielding Brokenness Comes By
Faith A Compassionate Pardoning Delights Victors On A Daily Basis.

At The Seams Where Life Inspirations Are The Strongest Unto Joyfulness With Robust And Great Mighty Seal Pushes Sturdily Forward. Overcoming All Conflicts Of Opposing Clashes And Resulting In A Daily Intact Unbroken Life's Pleasing Conquest.

At The Seams All Nations Of The Earth Come In Awe; Bowing Down
And Worshiping Our Maker Without Provocation In The Beauty Of
Holiness Giving Glory Honor Majesty And Endless Praise Unto THE
HOLY LAMB OF GOD! WORTHY IS THE LAMB! There Is Still Room
At The Overcomer's Cross For You!!!!

Songs Of Deliverance And Mercy!
Ps. 32:7, 8, 10, 11

When The Storms Of Life Are Raging Deep Within My Body, Heart And mine.
When Eerie Hopeless Darkness Covers The Long Weary Unearthly Time Of Day.
When Hurtful Sorrows Overlay Tiring The Responsible For Me To Daily Pray.
Watching Over Me, THOU Shall Compass Me About With Songs Of Deliverance And Mercy!
When Toughing JESUS Is All That Matters! Hallelujah!!! The Songs Joyfully Ringing Anew I WILL Sing! In The Joy Of THE LORD Is Our Added Strength To Be Found.

When I Can Not See Tomorrow I Bring Unto You Every Care Because You Gave Me The Songs.
When Health Possibilities Provided Are Exhausted And In My Old Age Made Short My Time.
When I Desire corrections Within All YOU DO. How Long Will Thou Hide THYSELF From Me?
Watching Over Me, THOU Shall Compass Me About With Songs Of Deliverance And Mercy!
When Toughing JESUS Is All That Matters! Hallelujah!!! The Songs Joyfully Ringing Anew I Will Sing! In The Joy Of THE LORD Is Our Added Strength To Be Found.

When I Inhabit THY Precious Presences The Chains Of This Life Fall Harmlessly Behind Me.

When The praises Go Up Passing Transitively Unto The HOLY ONE OF ISRAEL. I'll Soar Away. In All Things . . . Thank you LORD, Thank You Jesus, Thank You Holy Spirit!

When I'm In Your Presences Although I'm Weak THOU Art Strong. Sincerely Kneeing At The Cross! I Can Feel All Unbelief Being Removed And The Wounds Are Healed.

Watching Over Me, THOU Shall Compass Me About With Songs Of Deliverances, Mercy, Hope, Peace And Joy Unspeakable!

When Touching JESUS Is All That Matters! Hallelujah!!! The Songs Joyfully Ringing Anew I Will Sing! In The Joy Of Our LORD Is Our Daily Added Strength To Be Found!

Real Heartfelt Love In The Proven Holy Word Of God (Ps. 119) (The Way Of The Cross!)

Genuine Great Faithfulness Being One Pure Communication
all the way through,
O, The Holy Way God Has Consecrated Sacred To Cause Us
To Inherit Substance!
Mainstay Ever Steady Ever Certain Source Of Vital Lasting
fullness Of Joy's strength,
Our One And Only Stabled Enduring Prudence Cry From
Above Centered Wisdom!

Blameless Holy Blood Of The Testament And First Holy
Righteous Judgment Quicken,
O, Our New Covenant Calm Steady Believers Precept
Brightest Oil Lamp Of Living Hope!
A Stronghold Almightily Pronounced Statute Made Manifest
The FATHER Has Provided,
A Better Earnest New Covenant Unto Salvation Which Is
Christ In You The Hope Of Glory!

Our Steadfast Awesome Anchor Wondrous Compassion
"GOD SO LOVED", (Jn. 3:16)
JESUS . . . Our Redeemer Holy Word Of God Made Flesh
And Fullness Of The Glorious Gospel!

"IT IS FINISHED!" (THE WAY OF THE C R O S S !) "HE
IS RISEN!"

WAIT UPON THE LORD . . . Alleluia! Alleluia! Alleluia!
Thanksgiving Praise Unto THE LAMB OF GOD!
O, THAT HOLY AWESOME PLACE . . . WHERE OUR
LORD JESUS PRESENCE FILLS EVERY SONG!!!
AND OUR HOLY AWESOME PRAISES UNTO JESUS
GO ON AND ON AND ON . . . FOREVERMORE!!!

O Jerusalem Jerusalem Jerusalem

THE GENTILES SHALL SEE THY RIGHTEOUSNESS,
AND ALL KINGS THY GLORY:
AND THOU SHALL BE CALLED BY A NEW NAME,
WHICH THE MOUTH OF THE LORD SHALL NAME
AND SO SHALL THY GOD REJOICE OVER THEE!!!
(TILL HE ESTABLISH JERUSALEM A PRAISE IN THE EARTH)

BEHOLD THY SALVATION COMETH . . . O JERUSALEM!!!

Victory Unto Victory!!!
(Exo. 14:14 2 Cor. 12:9)

THE LORD IS NIGH UNTO ALL THEM WHO TRUST
HIM AND DEPART FROM EVERY EVIL WAY,
THE EYES OF ALL WHO WAIT UPON HIM TO SEE HIS
LOVINGKINDNESS O, SO HAPPY ARE THE
PEOPLE WHOSE GOD IS THE LORD. IT IS PLEASANT
TO KNOW THE JOY AND PEACE OF OUR
SALVATION . . . HE MADE A PROMISE HE GAVE EVERY
DROP OF BLOOD HE DIED ON THE CROSS
SO WE MIGHT BE FREE!!! I'M SO THANKFUL HIS
PRECIOUS REDEEMING BLOOD COVERS ME
TILL THERE BE NO MORE SIN!!! I'M IN THE BLOOD!!!
I'M IN THE BLOOD!!! I'M BLOOD
BOUGHT, IT IS FINISED!!! LOOKING UNTO JESUS
FAITH!!! WHICH IS CHRIST IN ME . . . THE
HOPE OF GLORY!!! SOME DAY I WILL LAY MY CROSS
DOWN AND GO HOME!!! ALLELUIA!!!

THE LORD IS GRACIOUS AND FULL OF COMPASSION
TO MAKE KNOWN HIS TENDER MERCIES,
WHEN THE MEEK FALLETH HE LIFTS THEM UP AND
RAISES UP THOSE WHO ARE BOWED
DOWN WHOSE GOD IS THE LORD, TO MAKE CLEAR
HIS EVERLASTING POWER AND HIS
MIGHTY ACTS . . . HE MADE A PROMISE HE GAVE
EVERY DROP OF BLOOD HE DIED ON THE

CROSS SO WE MIGHT BE FREE!!! I'M SO THANKFUL HIS PRECIOUS REDEEMING BLOOD COVERS ME TILL THERE BE NO MORE SIN!!! I'M IN THE BLOOD!!! I'M IN THE BLOOD!!! I'M BLOOD BOUGHT, IT IS FINISHED!!! LOOKING UNTO JESUS FAITH!!! WHICH IS CHRIST IN ME . . . THE HOPE OF GLORY!!! SOME DAY I WILL LAY MY CROSS DOWN AND GO HOME. ALLELUIA!!!

When Our Delight And Joy Is In Jesus
PSALM 37:3-5

(VOWED: I AM MY BELOVED'S AND MY BELOVED IS MINE. Song-2:16)

The Amplified Lesson intentionally Providing Stronger Faith And
Linked Together With Obedience To Do Good Increases Our Daily Cheerfulness And Our Daily Burdens Become Less Heavy.
When Our Delight And Joy Is In Jesus . . . Our Daily Righteousness.

Addressing Our Vowed Assured Desired Heart's Confidence and
Linked Together With Pleasure of Gratifications Increasing Our
Daily Self-sufficiency and Our Daily Fulfillment Comes to Pass.
When Our Delight And Joy Is In Jesus . . . Our Daily Fed Passion.

Knowing We Know Our Banners Are Sturdy And Time Is Coming
In Fullness Watching And Waiting Increasing A Richness Unique.
We Shall Behold Him The Holy Lamb Of God Holy One Of Israel.
When Our Delight And Joy Is In Jesus Lord Of lords King Of kings

Then Came The Morning In Jerusalem!
Heb. 10:20

An Appointed Time Of Liberation: For The Angel Of The Lord Came And Rolled Back The Stone And The Keepers When They Witnessed The Angel's Expression Begin To Shudder For Fear And Fail To The Earth As Dead Men. ISRAEL . . . THY GOD IS . . . AN AWESOME GOD!!! (Exo. 14:14)

Time Of Jubilation JESUS IS ALIVE!: JESUS IS RISEN! WOW!
JESUS Met With His Disciples And Told Them To Fear Not And His Disciples Fail At JESUS Feet And Worshiped Him. The Breaking News In Jerusalem Was Doubted By Some.

An Appointed Time Of Confidence: To Teach And Spread The Good News! Of The Glorious Gospel . . ."For God So Loved The World That He Gave His Only Begotten Son That Whosoever Believeth In Him Should Not Perish But Have Everlasting Life." One By One The Meek Have Come!

Happy 2008 Israel Sixtieth (Up To Jerusalem! ISA.62)

O, to stand upon THE MOUNT OF OLIVES where JESUS stood and
to attest first-hand The Genuiness Of JERUSALEM. Truly,
The Priceless Trip Of My Life Time!!! REMEMBRANCERS OF
JERUSALEM!!! ISA.62

The White Stone, JERUSALEM'S icon!!!
As A Matter Of Fact: It Is Against The Law
To Use Any Other Color Stone In The (Surface)
Construction Of Any Building In JERUSALEM.

When The Light Shines Upon JERUSALEM,
The White Stone Icon In Representation Of
THE Awesomeness Beauty Of Holiness Forms
An Inspiring Awe Golden Yellow Color Of Purity.

Appreciate And Be Grateful For . . .

(The Cross . . . Then Came The Morning!!! The angel rolled The stone away!!!)

JESUS . . . A BLAMELESS MAN . . .
O, THE distress of truth . . . To be accused untruly!!!
THE individual receiving . . . THY WILL BE DONE!!!
O, THE pain & tears, The misery, THE heartache!!!

THE scornfulness . . . When they said, HE IS ONLY A MAN!!!
The beatings, The bruises, THE strips, THE thrones, THE nails,

To Walk . . . THE WALK JESUS . . . WALKED!!! In Jerusalem That Day.
O, THE sufferings of CHRIST JESUS . . . Is So Hard To Comprehend!!!
THE CROSS . . . Then Came The Morning! In Jerusalem . . . The Angel
Rolled The Stone Away!!!*** JESUS IS ALIVE!!! HE IS RISEN!!!***

Appreciate And Be Grateful!!!
I COR. 15:51-58

(GIVING . . . THANKSGIVING PRAISE & WORSHIP ALWAYS!!!
LOOKING UNTO JESUS . . . THE SPOTLESS LAMB OF GOD!!!)

O, THE Endured Anguish Of THE Truth . . . To Be Accused Untruly!!!
O, THE Genuine Felt Awe THE Yielded Spirit . . . THY WILL BE DONE!!!!!
O, The Soreness Of Darkness THE Closing In . . . With No Comforter!!!
O, THE Pain, THE Sorrow & THE Tears, THE Misery, THE Heartache!!!!!
O, THE Lower Scornfulness . . . When They Said, "HE IS ONLY A MAN!!!"
Endured The Beatings THE Bruises, THE Strips, THE Thrones, THE Nails.

Via Dolorosa O, THE Blood Intact Path To Cavalry . . . No Turning Back!!!
O, THE Better Sacrificed THE Better Covenant The Better Revelation!!!

(TO Walk . . . THE WALK JESUS . . . WALKED!!! In Jerusalem That Day!!!

HE EXPERIENCED A REALISTIC AMAZING GRACE FOR YOU AND ME!!!
WILLINGLY HE GAVE WHAT ONLY HE COULD GIVE . . . H I M S E L F !!!)

O, THE Sufferings Of CHRIST JESUS . . . Is So Hard To Comprehend!!!
THE CROSS . . . It Is Finished!!! Then Came THE Morning! In Jerusalem . . .
THE Angel Rolled THE Stone Away!!! THE FATHER HAS PROVIDED!!!

JESUS IS ALIVE!!! HE HAS RISEN!!! O, THE Honor, THE Joy, THE Rest,
THE Hope, THE Glory Set Before JESUS . . . JESUS EYES ARE SHINING LIKE
FIRE, AS HIS BRIDE IS MAKING HERSELF, Ready To Be Revealed In THE
Last Time!!! WHO'S SUFFICIENCY IS OF GOD!!! WAIT UPON THE LORD.
THE DIVINE FATHER HAST PROVIDED!!! THE LION AND THE LAMB!!!
JESUS . . . THE LION OF JUDAH, THE LAMB OF GOD!!! AWESOMENESS!!!
THE Redeemed . . . SHALL BEHOLD HIM!!! Purchased . . . PAID IN FULL!!!

Jesus . . . lord Of New Life!!!

WHEN MY LIFE WAS BROKEN AND IN RUIN . . .
JESUS INTERCESSION GAVE ME HIS NEW LIFE!!!

WHEN I HAD NO STRENGTH . . .
JESUS GAVE ME HIS STRENGTH!!!

WHEN I HAD NO FAMILY . . .
JESUS GAVE ME HIS FAMILY!!!

WHEN I HAD NO HOPE . . .
JESUS GAVE ME HIS HOPE!!!

WHEN I HAD NO DIRECTION . . .
JESUS GAVE ME HIS DIRECTION!!!

WHEN I FOUND JESUS WAS ALL I HAVE . . .
JESUS TURNED OUT TO BE ALL I NEED!!!

WHEN I DAILY YIELD MY HEART UNTO JESUS . . .
JESUS DAILY OPENS HIS HEART UNTO ME!!!

ALL TOGETHER MY BELOVED IS MINE . . .
ALL TOGETHER I AM MY BELOVED!!!

The Way Of Holiness!!!

(I'm forever changed BY THE PRECIOUS REDEEMING BLOOD OF CHRIST JESUS!!!)

THE LORD SHALL CAUSE RIGHTEOUSNESS AND PRAISE TO SPRING UP AS THE EARTH BRINGS FORTH BUD, AS A FLOURISHED GARDEN SOWN. AND A HIGHWAY, AND A WAY, SHALL BE THERE.

IT SHALL BE CALLED . . . THE WAY OF HOLINESS!!! NO IMPURITY SHALL PASS OVER AND NO FOOL. ONLY THE REDEEMED SHALL WALK THERE!!! ONE AND ALL RANSOMED WHITE AS SNOW!!!

THE PRESENCE OF THE LORD WILL FILL EVERY SONG AS THE REDEEMED RETURN UNTO ZION. THE SONG SHALL GO ON CONTINUALLY EVER AND FOREVERMORE WITH A EVERLASTING JOY.

Never Before

NEVER BEFORE HAS ONE MAN, SPOKE LIKE THIS WITH SURE
AUTHORITY AND TOTAL CONTROL COMMAND, IN HIS VOICE.
NEVER BEFORE HAS A MAN SPOKE SO COMPASSIONATELY IN
STEADFAST RICHNESS AND REDEEMING POWER, IN HIS VOICE.

JESUS IS WORTHY OF ALL PRAISE!!!

NEVER BEFORE HAS ONE MAN, JOY COMPLETELY TURNED THE
WORLD UP SIDE DOWN WITH HIS NEW WAY OF LIFE, WISDOM.
NEVER BEFORE HAS ONE MAN HUMBLED HIMSELF OVERALL TO
REPURCHASE MAN, MAGNIFYING HIS UTMOST WORTHINESS.

JESUS IS WORTHY OF ALL PRAISE!!!

NEVER BEFORE HAD ONE MAN, PURIFIED HIS ENTIRE LIFE ON
THIS EARTH WITHOUT WRONGDOING AND WITHOUT SHAME.
NEVER BEFORE HAD ONE MAN BEEN EXALTED TO SET AT THE

RIGHT HAND OF THE THRONE OF GOD, NOT EVEN THE ANGELS.

JESUS IS WORTHY OF ALL PRAISE!!!

THERE IS NO OTHER!!!

I'm In The Blood
Gal. 6:14-Rom. 8 (Isa. 53 . . . via Dolorosa)

(SOME GRAND DAY, I WILL LAY DOWN MY CROSS, AND GO HOME!!!)

NO CONDEMNATION . . . IT IS FINISHED, I'M SO THANKFUL, I'M COVERED
IN THE PRECIOUS REDEEMING BLOOD OF CHRIST JESUS. CHRIST JESUS
BLOOD FLOWS DEEPER THAN ALL MY SINS. OVER AND DONE WITH, AS
EACH MORNING BREAKS, IT'S BEEN MERCY ALL THE WAY, WASHING ME
WHITE AS SNOW. VIRTUE CAPABILITY, AWESOME . . . I'M BLOOD BOUGHT,
TILL THERE BE NO MORE SIN!!!. I'M FOREVERMORE, THE FRUIT OF THE
OLD RUGGED CROSS, CHRIST JESUS DID NOT SUFFER & DIE IN VAIN.

NO UNFASTENING . . . SET & SEALED, CAN'T BE UNDONE, NOTHING CAN
UNDO WHAT CHRIST JESUS PRECIOUS REDEEMING BLOOD HAS EARLIER
PREPARED FOR ME. THE ASSETS WHEREWITHAL WEALTH OF EACH AND
EVER ONE SOW & SEALED TO REAPING. ENDLESS COMPASSIONS FREELY

FLOWING TO WATER THE GARDEN. BLESSINGS UNTO ALL WHO BLESS
ISRAEL. PRAY FOR JERUSALEM. I'M FOREVERMORE, THE FRUIT OF THE
OLD RUGGED CROSS, CHRIST JESUS DID NOT SUFFER & DIE IN VAIN.

NO TERMINAING . . . CAN'T BE DEFIED, NOTHING CAN CHALLENGE WHAT
CHRIST JESUS PRECIOUS REDEEMING BLOOD DEFENDS ME FROM AT ALL
TIMES, SURROUNDED BY THE BLOOD OF CHRIST JESUS., COMING IN AND
GOING OUT, PERSERVED, AND SHELTERED, AWESOME CONTAINED SAFE
IN CHRIST JESUS!!! "I'M IN THE BLOOD! I'M IN THE BLOOD! I'M IN THE
BLOOD.!" LET GOD BE MAGNIFIED. I'M FOREVERMORE, THE FRUIT OF
THE OLD RUGGED CROSS, CHRIST JESUS DID NOT SUFFER & DIE IN VAIN.

Daily Results Of Hope And Blessings Over The Years

THAT MY WEAKNESS AND INADEQUACY BECOMES JESUS OPPORTUNITY
TO HELP . . . WHEN I WAS BROUGHT LOW, AND I DID NOT EVEN CONTAIN
STRENGTH TO STAND, I FELL FLAT ON MY FACE. THAT'S WHEN JESUS
HELPED ME!!! THE SPIRIT ITSELF BEARING WITNESS WITH MY SPIRIT,
SAYING, YOU ARE MY SON, I WILL NEVER FORGET THAT DAY WHEN MY
LIFE . . . JESUS CHANGED!!! SO THAT, THE POWER OF CHRIST MAY REST
UPON ME. I'M COUNTING MY MANY BLESSINGS, LOOKING UNTO JESUS!!!

THAT MY TRUST DAILY BE FAITHFUL AND TRUE, IN THE LORD CHRIST
JESUS . . . WHO IS PERFORMING ACTS OF HIS DIVINE RIGHTEOUSNESS ON
THE WAY TO ACHIEVING ALL HE HAS PREPARED FOR ME. I'M REACHING
UNTO JESUS SUFFICIENCY AND A BETTER POSSESSION . . . ALL MY NEEDS
ARE DAILY ADVANCED IN HIS GRANDEUR'S LIKENESS AND EXCEPTIONAL

COMMANDMENT'S DIGNITY, SO THAT, THE POWER
OF CHRIST MAY REST
UPON ME. I'M COUNTING MY MANY BLESSINGS,
LOOKING UNTO JESUS!!!

THAT MY HOLDING FORTH THE WORD OF
GOD . . . BEING NOT FRUITLESS,
AND THAT I HAVE NOT RUN THIS RACE IN VAIN,
NOR LABOURED IN VAIN
BUT OUT OF WEAKNESS, I HAVE GROWN STRONG
IN THE POWER OF THE
SPIRIT AFFIRMING, THE LORD CHRIST JESUS
ALONE CAN FULLY SATISFY
MY EARNEST HEART SALVATION INCLUSIVE IN
HIM: WHICH IS CHRIST IN
ME THE HOPE OF GLORY!!! SO THAT, THE POWER
OF CHRIST MAY REST
UPON ME. I'M COUNTING MY MANY BLESSINGS,
LOOKING UNTO JESUS!!!

Daily Inspired

(ONLY JESUS CAN RAISE ME UP . . .
TO MORE THAN . . . I CAN BE)

AS MORNING BREAKS I LOOK UNTO JESUS FOR MY STRENGTH
THIS DAY, FEELING JESUS WARMTH BY MEANS OF THE HOLY
SPIRITS HELP. ENCOURAGING ME AND ANEWING MY DAILY
INSPIRATION; FOR ME TO FOLLOW FIRMLY AFTER JESUS JOYFUL
AND STEADFASTLY; NOT FOR A SEASON BUT FOREVERMORE.

THE SAME AS, WALKING IN JESUS LIGHT SEEING EXPLANATION
THAT MY ONE MORE DAYLIGHT, JESUS HAS FIXED FIRMLY THE
EVERLASTING FORTIFICATION, IN THE BEAUTY OF HIS
HOLINESS A PRESENCE TOKEN OF INSPIRATION; FOR ME TO
FOLLOW FIRMLY AFTER JESUS JOYFULLY AND STEADFASTLY;
NOT FOR A SEASON BUT FOREVERMORE.

AS I TAKE UP MY CROSS AND CONTINUING DAILY, FULLY
PERSUADED THAT MY SUFFERINGS ARE NOT WORTHY TO BE

COMPARED WITH THE BEAUTY JESUS CONTINUALLY UNVEILS
IN THE MIDST OF INSPIRATION; FOR ME TO FOLLOW FIRMLY
AFTER JESUS JOYFULLY AND STEADFASTLY; NOT FOR A
SEASON BUT FOREVERMORE.

SOME GRAND DAY MY CROSS I WILL LAY DOWN, AND GO HOME
TO A PLACE WHERE MY BELOVED JESUS PRAISES GO ON AND
ON AND ON.(O, MY DEEPEST LONGING . . . TO HEAR JESUS SAY
UNTO ME "WELL DONE") AND THE SHOUTS OF JOY AND
GLADNESS FILLS THE UNVERSE; UNTO THE HOLY HOLY HOLY
LAMB OF GOD WHO IS ALL TOGETHER LOVELY!!!

(((((((EVEN SO . . . LORD JESUS >>>>>>> COME)))))))

Your Heart Soars In Jerusalem, ISA. 51:

THANK YOU LORD . . . ALL TOGETHER LOVELY FOR SENDING YOUR DEARLY
BELOVED SON.

THANK YOU JESUS . . . GREAT COST FOR WILLINGLY DOING YOUR DIVINE
FATHER'S WILL.

THANK YOU HOLY SPIRIT . . . COMFORTER FOR DAILY INSPIRING ME AND
HELPING ME STAND.

IN ALL THINGS . . . THANK YOU LORD, THANK YOU JESUS, THANK YOU HOLY SPIRIT.

THE SHOUT OF EL—SHADDAI . . . EVEN SO . . . LORD JESUS >>>
COME . . . COME LORD JESUS . . . AMEN

(NOTHING BUT THE PRECIOUS BLOOD OF JESUS.)

IT'S ALL ABOUT YOU . . . J E S U S!!!

IN FAITH AND HOPE . . . I DAILY LIFT UP THE EYES
OF MY HEART

WATCHING AND WAITING. EVEN SO . . . LORD JESUS >>> COME.

MY DESIRE IS TO BE GREATLY SETTLED IN . . . J E S U S!!!
HIS BLOOD BOUGHT . . . HIS REDEEMED . . . HIS OVERCOMER!!!

THAT ONE AND ALL HAVE TO ENTER THROUGHT . . . H I M!!!
GO IN IF THEY ARE LOOKING FOR OR, WANT TO FIND . . . ME!!!

WHILE I DAILY EAGERLY LIVE BY FAITH FRUIT OF THE CROSS!!!
IN THE PRECIOUS BLOOD OF JESUS THOU ART MY HIDING PLACE.

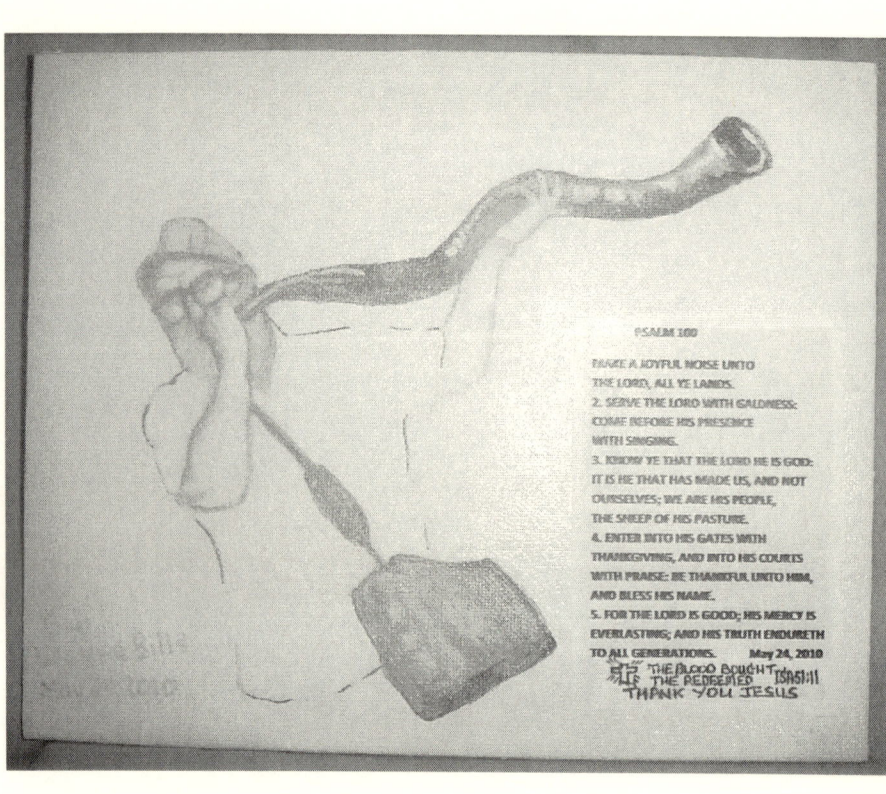

THE DAY OF THE LORD (JUSTNESS)

I THESS. 4:16-18

(FOR THE LORD HIMSELF . . . SHALL DESCEND FROM HEAVEN WITH A SHOUT)

There Is Not Anything . . . To Weight Against.
Doesn't Matter What Objection . . . No Opposition.
THERE IS NO WISDOM AGAINST . . . EL SHADDAI!!!

There Is Not Anywhere . . . To Take Flight.
Doesn't Matter Where . . . Tryster Escape.
THERE IS NO WISDOM AGAINST . . . EL SHADDAI!!!

There Is Not Anyplace . . . Defensibly Secured.
Doesn't Matter What Concealed Place . . . Can't Hide.
THERE IS NO WISDOM AGAINST . . . EL SHADDAI!!!

THE SHOUT OF EL SHADDAI . . .
EVEN SO . . . LORD JESUS >>> COME
COME . . . LORD JESUS . . . AMEN